JOURNEY

ADVANCE PRAISE

"Journey's story is one of redemption – for us and for wolves. Beckie Elgin has done a wonderful job telling the story and helping us better understand wolves. That's important if we're to avoid repeating past mistakes. No matter your age, you'll enjoy this book immensely – and likely learn something along the way. I sure did!"

Rob Klavins
Northeast Oregon Field Coordinator for Oregon Wild

"Beckie writes with a contagious passion that appeals to the young in all of us. A factual, naturalist style that only comes from having lived it...with the wolves! She is truly helping us all better understand and appreciate wildlife and the natural world and most importantly, how all the parts fit together into one complete story."

Joe Kreuzman
Wildlife Tracker and Co-Founder and Director of Coyote Trails School of Nature

"Young readers will fall in love with Elgin's animal-eye view of Journey, a wolf whose wanderlust carriers him across western landscapes and into human hearts. Journey teaches us about predators and their prey—and the curiosity streak and survival drive we all share."

DeLene Beeland
Author of *The Secret World of Red Wolves*

JOURNEY

The Amazing Story of OR-7, the Oregon Wolf that Made History

Beckie Elgin

INKWATER PRESS

Edited by David Aretha, Tim Kerlin, and Holly Tri

Cover and interior design by Michael Ebert

Woods by Sebastian Engler | unsplash.com
OR-7 (Journey) from the US Fish and Wildlife Service

Publisher: Inkwater Press | www.inkwaterpress.com

Paperback
ISBN-13 978-1-62901-399-2 | ISBN-10 1-62901-399-4

Kindle
ISBN-13 978-1-62901-409-8 | ISBN-10 1-62901-409-5

ePub
ISBN-13 978-1-62901-410-4 | ISBN-10 1-62901-410-4

Printed in the U.S.A.

3 5 7 9 10 8 6 4 2

A portion of the proceeds of this book go to support Oregon Wild in their tireless efforts to protect wolves.

DEDICATION

To my own much loved pack, Hannah, Megan, and Dylan. And to Hansel and Gretel, Taurus, Gray-boy, Akela, and the other wolves of my past.

Hansel at three years old.

CONTENTS

PREFACE

This is the story of a wolf, one who became famous because of the long and remarkable journey he made. But this very special wolf doesn't know he is famous. Known as OR-7, or Journey, he lives the life of a regular wolf, searching for food, playing with his family, and doing his best to stay away from humans.

In this book, we come to learn about Journey in two ways. First is through the eyes of the wolf himself. These sections are based on what scientists and others know about Journey and other wolves; however, the facts are enhanced with touches of well-informed imagination. This point of view gives us a sense of what it must be like to be a wild wolf, how wolves use their senses to survive, how they struggle to find food, and how they interact with each other.

Second, we learn about Journey and his kind through the viewpoint of wolf biologists and advocates who endeavor to understand and protect *Canis lupus*. A brief history of wolves in our country is also offered as a way of better comprehending their current situation. A great deal of information has been gathered about wolves through observation and scientific studies. Yet despite what we know and what we can imagine about the wandering wolf known as Journey, much of his life remains a mystery, as it should.

AUTHOR'S NOTE

In September of 2011, I was in northeastern Oregon for a weeklong stay at the Imnaha House, a rustic lodge where writers gather to work on their craft. The road to the Imnaha House is a pot-holed gravel lane that stretches for miles through sparsely inhabited ranchlands. Cattle have the right of way there, and a couple of times, I had to stop my car and wait for small herds of them to cross the road, something they were in no hurry to do. As I drove, I scanned the wide-open horizon for wolves, hoping to catch sight of the Imnaha pack that resided there. But wolves are much more elusive than cattle, and I didn't see a one.

When I finally arrived at the lodge, next to the Imnaha River and barely visible behind a thick row of fir trees, my car was bumping over the gravel road even more than usual. When I got out to unload, I saw the reason why: my rear passenger tire was losing air like a balloon that had been poked with a thumbtack. No matter; I had arrived. The tire could wait.

After an inspiring week at the Imnaha House (and a new tire!), I headed home to Southern Oregon. But this time I didn't feel like I was traveling alone. I'd been told that OR-7, a young gray wolf of the Imnaha pack, had dispersed a few weeks earlier and was headed in the same direction I was. I'll never forget the feeling of driving along the rural roads and then the highways, imagining OR-7 running alongside me, safe within the cover of the forest. Of course, I didn't see him, but I felt his presence just the same.

This experience prompted me to begin writing about wolves, especially wolves in Oregon. They were a fledging species in my state, having just begun to repopulate the area after decades of their absence. My hope was to do my part to raise awareness of the importance of wolves to the environment and how we humans need to let them be.

Besides feeling a connection with the wolves of Oregon, I'd had the good fortune of growing up with them. My father, Robert Elgin, was director of a small zoo in Des Moines, Iowa. He worked hard to raise funds to create large and naturalistic enclosures for the animals he loved. As his daughter, I worked hard in my own way, which was primarily taking care of the wolves. When I was twelve years old, I was given the challenging job of taming a pair of very frightened three-month-old wolf cubs that, until arriving at our facility, had never been handled by humans. That summer I spent all day sitting in the pen with the wolves, who were named Hansel and Gretel because they seemed as lost as those two children. Eventually, the cubs forgot their fear of me and allowed me to stroke their soft coats and take them on long walks. I grew to respect and love these animals, at the same time realizing they were much different canines than our black Labrador at home. Wolves always keep their wildness, I learned, and as gentle as they are, they are not pet material.

As the years passed, I raised other wolves at the zoo, some of them offspring of Hansel and Gretel. I also accompanied my dad as he spoke to various groups in the community. My job was to hold a wolf on a leash while my father explained to the audience that *Canis lupus* is not the monster it is portrayed to be in fairy tales, but rather an intelligent and sensitive animal that deserves our protection.

Being exposed to wolves as a girl was a gift I will be forever grateful for. There was magic in those years of my life, a magic that allowed me to believe I could tame a pair of virtually wild wolves and that nothing would stand in my way. I see this same enthusiasm and optimism in young people today, and it is out of respect for these qualities that I wrote this book for them.

CHAPTER ONE

The Beginning

He awoke to the distant sound of howling, stood on wobbly legs, and shook the dirt from his short, gray coat. His littermates still slept, their blunt noses buried in the warmth of each other's fur to ward off the morning chill. The long climb out of the den wasn't easy for the three-week-old wolf pup, but he was the adventurer of the litter, already curious about the world outside. Sharp claws scrambled on stones and packed earth as he climbed up the narrow tunnel. Finally, he reached the opening of the den his mother had dug a month earlier in anticipation of the birth of her litter.

The pup blinked as sunlight touched his eyes, and he took a deep breath of the fresh mountain air. For the first time in his life, he gazed at the dense forest around him. The broad trunks of the ponderosa pine and Douglas fir filled his view, and then he saw the sudden shifting of leaves on an aspen as the wind stirred. His nostrils opened wide to take in the surrounding scents. The young wolf did not yet know what the smells were, but they excited him. He noticed a familiar scent, one that carried with it warm milk and a gentle tongue. He heard the sound of a twig cracking and spotted his mother trotting through the forest toward the mouth of the den. She saw him and quickened her pace.

The mother wolf approached, her coat steel-gray like his, and the pup rushed to her, whining. The two licked each other's muzzles and

* *Some wolf dens are simply shallow holes in the ground, but some are quite elaborate. Gordon Haber, a biologist who studied wolves at Denali National Park in Alaska, explored den areas that had a network of deep tunnels, as well as resting and viewing areas above ground. Some dens he studied have been used by wolves for hundreds, perhaps thousands, of years.*

their tails wagged. The pup's tail wagged so fast that he nearly lost his balance and toppled over. His mother gently nudged him in the direction of the den. He tried to hold his ground, wanting to stay outside and explore the vast forest, but the larger wolf won out, and the pup's seven-pound body tumbled down the slope of the tunnel.

The den* echoed with the whines of the blue-eyed babies as they pounced on their mother. The gray pup joined in, and they all scrambled in the cramped, dark space, trampling each other as they greeted her. There was a medley of high-pitched squeaks, a flashing of pink tongues, and a furious wagging of tails. When the welcome ceremony was complete, the adult wolf dropped to her side, and all six pups, most gray like her, a few black like their father, rushed to her belly, pushing each other aside in an effort to feed. The babies locked on, and their tiny paws pressed against their mother's body, working the milk down as they suckled. She sighed and laid her head on the floor of the den. Her young nursed as she drifted into a sound sleep, worn out by the morning's hunt.

The adventurous gray pup finished feeding first. He took a few slow steps toward the entry of the den. His round belly, full of milk, nearly touched the ground. He walked a few feet before he became too sleepy to go on, then his short legs gave way,

PHOTO: OREGON DEPARTMENT OF FISH AND WILDLIFE (ODFW). MAY 30, 2012.

Pups from the Wenaha pack of northeastern Oregon at approximately six weeks of age.

and he plopped down, gazing longingly at the bright oval of sunlight that shone through the door of the tunnel. Later, when not so full and not so drowsy, he would explore again. But not now. His eyes closed and he fell fast asleep.

THE CELEBRITY

This inquisitive wolf pup was born deep in the Wallowa-Whitman National Forest of northeastern Oregon in mid-April of 2009, among one of the first litters born in the state in more than sixty years. Although he was an average-looking wolf, raised with his brothers and sisters far from the eyes of humans, this young animal soon became one of the most famous wolves in history. He is known as Journey, and for a very good reason.

Journey left his pack as a two-year-old and made for faraway lands. This is not unusual behavior for young wolves, but this curious creature traveled much farther than most. Within a few months, he traversed hundreds of miles to become the first wolf in Western Oregon in more than seventy years. As if this wasn't enough of a jaunt, Journey then wandered into California, a state that had not seen wild wolves for almost a century. All in all, he logged over four thousand air miles before settling down in his new home in southwestern Oregon, where he finally found what he was searching for.**

Newspapers, television stations, and the Internet told the world about Journey's remarkable travels. People cheered for him from the sidelines, hoping for his safety from all the dangers wolves face. Journey became an inspiration to many, as well as an ambassador that taught us much about the ways of wolves.

** If you were to travel the same route as Journey in a car, an airplane, or on a bicycle, you would not have gone nearly so many miles. But wild animals don't travel like we do; they don't stick to roads and they aren't always focused on going from one point to another. Journey made many, many detours along the way, and this is why he traveled so many miles. Also, due to how they are measured, one air mile equals 6,080 feet, while a land mile is 5,280 feet.

THE FAMILY

Not so long ago, wolves lived throughout all of Oregon. In fact, they roamed nearly everywhere in the United States. But early European settlers brought with them fears of the wolf, created in part by religious teachings and carried on in old tales such as "Little Red Riding Hood" and "Peter and the Wolf." There was some basis to their fears, as wolves in Europe did at times prey on humans. But many of these attacks occurred because the wolves were rabid. Rabies was common until Louis Pasteur discovered the vaccine for this deadly disease in 1885.

Early settlers were intimidated by the North American wilderness and tried to conquer it by destroying forests, damming rivers, and killing wild animals. Of course, hundreds of thousands of Native American people died as well, either intentionally at the hands of the newcomers or from the many diseases the settlers brought with them.

In these early times of our country, wolves were shot, poisoned, trapped, and even tortured by settlers. The United States government and the individual states joined in, offering bounties for wolf pelts. Some of the bounties were as valuable as a month's salary for many, making it tempting to kill wolves. With all of these forces working

Cowboys roping a gray wolf in Wyoming, 1887.

PHOTO: LIBRARY OF CONGRESS.

against them, the wolf population was soon in sharp decline.

In the western states, people also killed vast numbers of ungulates, or hoofed animals. This was done for the meat, to clear land for farming, and sometimes simply for sport. The government ordered entire herds of bison shot as a way of taking food away from Native Americans, who for centuries had survived by eating and using the hides of these huge creatures. Bison were also killed to provide food for workers as they built railroads to improve transportation to the

Hunter with six wolves killed in or around Yellowstone National Park, 1902.

West. Bison and other ungulates are the natural prey of wolves, and when food was no longer plentiful, the canines became hungry. Some began to hunt cattle and sheep. This created problems for ranchers and farmers and gave people even more reason to wage war against wolves.

This war was fought for many years. Wolves did not stand a chance against the guns, traps, and poisons used against them. By the early 1800s, they had been killed off in the eastern part of the United States. By the 1900s, wolves were gone from the Midwestern states, except for small populations in Minnesota and Michigan. Eventually, they were removed, one by one, from the West as well. Experts believe that approximately one million wolves were killed in the US during the nineteenth and twentieth centuries.

PHOTO: FROM A. R. HARDING'S WOLF AND COYOTE TRAPPING, 1909.

Wolf hunter with hunting dogs and wolf pelts, 1909.

* The term keystone species comes from an old architectural word. The top stone of an arch is called the keystone. If it is removed, the arch falls apart. Keystone species are animals that hold a crucial role in their environment. When these species are removed, the environment may not fall apart, but it certainly changes. An animal does not need to be a predator to be considered a keystone species. Beaver fit the criteria. They gnaw down trees, which allows for new ponds and meadows to develop. And their dams provide shelter and food sources for many other species. Other keystone species include sharks, elephants, bison, brown bears, gray whales, and lions.

** Ancient Inuit saying: "Where the wolves hunt, the caribou herds are healthy."

While some were happy the wolves were gone, many weren't. Most of us respect wolves and believe they have a right to live in their natural environment. We enjoy having the opportunity to see them in the wild and hear the music of their mournful howl beneath an open sky. As social creatures ourselves, we appreciate how wolves live in family groups and take care of each other. We also know that dogs, a species very close to us, evolved from wolves.

Canis lupus also plays an important role in maintaining a healthy ecosystem. Trophic cascades, a theory that helps us understand this role, refers to the complex mechanism of nature in which predators affect the population and behavior of their prey. This effect trickles, or cascades, down to other animals, plants, and the environment in ways we are just beginning to understand.

As keystone predators,* wolves contribute to the trophic cascades cycle. By hunting hoofed animals, they help prevent overpopulation of these species. When ungulate numbers are not controlled by wild predators, the hoofed animals tend to eat too much vegetation, which can be harmful to the environment. For example, elk and deer enjoy browsing on trees that grow alongside streams and rivers, including willow, aspen, and cottonwood. But when these trees become overbrowsed, they die off. After the trees are gone, there is nothing left to shade the waterway, making the area too warm for some types of fish. Birds and other animals lose cover to hide in and places to raise their young. Beavers, another essential species that helps protect waterways, no longer have material to build their dams with. The cycle continues to cascade, affecting many aspects of the environment.

Wolves are beneficial to the natural world in other ways as well. They are opportunistic hunters and will hunt any prey they can catch. They even eat carrion. Weak and sick animals are easier to capture, so wolves consume a lot of them, which promotes healthier populations.** The creatures they kill provide food for other wildlife, including coyotes, bears, and ravens. Even insects feast on the carcasses.

Amaroq Weiss works as the West Coast Wolf Organizer for a nonprofit conservation organization called Center for Biological Diversity. Amaroq, whose name means wolf, has always loved these animals, and in order to help protect them, she studied first as a biologist and then as a lawyer. Amaroq explains the importance of wolves in a way that everyone, including sports fans, can understand: "Over millions of years, wolves have been the driving force that pushed deer, elk, and caribou to become so fast, so strong, so agile, that they are a match for the wolf. No one animal can be said to shape nature on its own, to exert the sole balancing force on the landscape, but if wild nature were an athletic event, the wolf would be crowned as its most valuable player."

Because of the research that has proven the value of wolves, as well as the fact that most people want them in the ecosystem, plans were made to reintroduce wolves into Yellowstone National Park and central Idaho in 1995 and 1996. After years of hard work and legal battles, sixty-six wild wolves from Canada were captured by biologists and transported to their new homes.***

PHOTO: NATIONAL PARK SERVICE

*** *Wolf released into pen at Yellowstone National Park in February, 1997. This is an example of "rewilding," which is a movement that attempts to reverse the human-caused destruction of the natural world by reintroducing native animals to places they once roamed. There are rewilding efforts going on across the globe, including one that hopes to bring wolves back to Britain, where they have not lived since the 1700s.*

PHOTO: US NATIONAL ARCHIVES.

* *North America's deepest river gorge, Hells Canyon, is nearly 2,000 feet deeper than the Grand Canyon. It is 125 miles long, forty miles of which is more than one mile deep. The Nez Perce (known to themselves as the Nimiipuu) were the first people to settle in the Hells Canyon area. Legend says a coyote used a long stick to dig out the canyon in order to provide a safe place for their people to live. In May of 1877, Chief Joseph's band of Nez Perce had to leave their homelands or face life on a reservation. They journeyed down the expanse of Hells Canyon and crossed the broad Snake River into Idaho. The Nez Perce eluded capture until forty miles from the Canadian border, where they were forced to surrender. Here, Chief Joseph is said to have voiced his famous words, "From where the sun now stands, I will fight no more forever."*

The wolves in Yellowstone and central Idaho found plenty of game to hunt. They formed new packs and their numbers grew.

More than three million people visit Yellowstone National Park each year. Yellowstone is one of the few places in the world where nearly all of the species native to the area still live together, coexisting in a natural way. Visitors line up alongside park roads with binoculars and spotting scopes. Many see bear, elk, bison, and deer, and since the reintroduction, some lucky folks catch sight of the elusive wolf, although usually from a long distance.

The wolves released in central Idaho did well also, although without the fanfare their Yellowstone pack mates received. Their numbers increased and they began to seek new territory. In January of 2008, a gray female from Idaho's Timberline pack swam across the Snake River, which flows within the deep Hells Canyon,* which divides Idaho from Oregon. When this young gray wolf crossed the river, she shook herself dry, not knowing that her swim had carried her to northeastern Oregon. She was eventually captured and collared by biologists and given the official name of OR-2, indicating that she was the second wolf collared in Oregon. Soon, another wolf, a large, black male, was located in the same area, collared and dubbed OR-4. He and OR-2 (also known as Sophie) found each other and joined forces, producing their first litter in 2008. Their family was called the Imnaha pack, sharing the name of the Imnaha River, which flows through their territory. Our curious little gray wolf pup came from the second litter born to this pack.

PHOTO: ODFW, JULY 9, 2011.

OR-2 was the second wolf collared in Oregon. Here she is with OR-4 and pups from two different litters.

PHOTO: ODFW, MAY 19, 2011.

OR-4 with collar and ear tags for quick identification.

CHAPTER TWO

Growing Up

It was mid-June and hot. The sun's rays worked their way between the bright green leaves of the aspen trees and shone on the gray pup. He awoke, stood up, and shook, tossing off bits of dirt from his coat. He panted, pink tongue dry, as he trotted the short distance to the creek. His littermates had already gathered there, also hot and thirsty. The young wolves stood side by side as they took in great mouthfuls of the cool, clear water.

The litter had grown a great deal in the first two months of their lives. They weighed an average of eighteen pounds each and stood almost a foot high at their shoulders. They no longer nursed, and large, sturdy adult teeth would soon replace their milk teeth. Their blue eyes were gradually changing to amber. Each pup had been born with its own distinct personality. This personality helped each serve its role in the family group. A cub might grow up to be a breeding adult or the wolf that watches over a new litter while the mother wolf goes off on a hunt. As the pups wrestled and played, their personalities shone through. Some liked to lead the others, a few were content to follow, while some hung out in the middle. They communicated with each other in wolf talk, using body language, glances, growls, whines, and howls. Sometimes, sharp teeth were used to get the point across. During their frequent periods of roughhousing, the young wolves also practiced skills that taught them to become efficient hunters.

The gray pup was a playful one. He quenched his thirst then bowed down with his hind end in the air, tail wagging, inviting the others to play. This began a wild game of chase across the shallow creek. Back and forth the brothers and sisters ran. When one pup was caught, the others wrestled it down, pulling at its ears and tail with their teeth. The youngsters rolled alongside the creek, enjoying the coolness of the mud. Soon, the lighter pups were nearly as dark as their black-coated littermates.

Busy with their antics, the pups didn't notice when their parents came around a bend in the creek and joined them. The adult wolves, the male black and the female gray, plopped down on the grass. The youngsters ran to them and, still filled with the joy of play, jumped on the big wolves, pulling at their fur and licking their faces. The parents rolled over and let their offspring have their fun.

When the father wolf had had enough of being chewed on, he stood to walk away. The pups swarmed around him, licking at his muzzle. This told the adult wolf that the young wolves were hungry, so he regurgitated, depositing a pile of partially digested elk meat on the grass. The pups gulped it down, growling and snapping at each other to make sure they got their share. Two of the more timid youngsters slunk back, barely getting a mouthful. The mother wolf regurgitated as well, and there was enough food for the whole litter.

PHOTO: ODFW TRAIL CAMERA, JULY 2014.

Pups from northeastern Oregon's Mount Emily pack.

The pups were full and sleepy once again. They found shady spots in the forest or dug into the soil to uncover the cool, moist dirt beneath the surface. Soon, they settled down for an afternoon nap. The adults rested too, but with their eyes half-open to watch over their young.

A pup from the Wenaha pack.

A WOLF BIOLOGIST

A nature lover from a young age, Roblyn Brown covered the walls of her bedroom with posters of birds and animals. After school, she would enter the front door of her Ohio home, grab her binoculars, and head out the back door to search for wildlife. Although Roblyn didn't live in a wilderness area, she discovered all types of creatures in the fields and wetlands near her home.

Roblyn's love of nature led her to study animals and the environment. She took science courses in high school, then attended college and earned a degree in zoology. After graduating, Roblyn worked in several locations on various wildlife projects. She studied grizzly bears at Jasper National Park in Alberta, Canada, and in Colorado she worked with cougars and snowshoe hares. In 2009 Roblyn moved to Oregon to research bighorn sheep for the Oregon Department of Fish and Wildlife. A year later, she was hired to be the department's Assistant Wolf Coordinator.

When Roblyn moved to Oregon, wolves were settling in the state as well. Sophie, her mate, OR-4, and their pups made up the Imnaha pack. Other wolves had formed a pack north of the Imnaha area. They were known as the Wenaha pack. Oregon, with its vast acres of forests, hills, and open plains, was once again a haven for wolves. Roblyn and Russ Morgan, the Wolf Coordinator for Oregon, would keep busy overseeing the state's wolves.

One way to study these animals and keep track of them is with the use of special collars. In order to place these collars, biologists trap wild wolves using a rubber-lined foothold trap or they shoot them from a helicopter with a gun that holds a tranquilizer dart. Inside the tranquilizer dart is medication that is released when it comes in contact with its target. This medication anesthetizes the animal, much like a person who is undergoing surgery. While the wolf is under sedation, biologists place a collar around the animal's neck. Secured on many of the collars is a small global positioning system (GPS) unit that receives signals transmitted by satellites orbiting earth. Location information stored in the GPS unit is periodically uploaded via satellite and emailed to a computer, where it shows up as dots on a map on the screen. These dots tell the biologist where the collared wolf is traveling.

The collars also use a VHF system, either alone or with the GPS. VHF stands for very high frequency, and this method transmits a signal that is picked up by an antenna either on the ground or in an airplane. The benefit of using both systems is that after the GPS battery wears out, in about three years, the wolf can still be tracked with the use of the VHF. However, a biologist must be close to the animal, holding a metal antenna, to pick up the VHF signal.

While the wolf is sedated, the biologists do much more than

PHOTO: ODFW, MARCH 24, 2014.

Roblyn Brown with a tranquilized wolf from the Snake River pack.

place the collar. They weigh the animal, take blood samples, measure its teeth, and check its overall condition. They keep detailed notes of their findings, and this data is used to help gain a better understanding of wolves. All of this must be done before the wolf begins to awaken from its no doubt restless nap.

Russ Morgan using a VHF antenna to search for a wolf.

 ## FIRST HUNT

The elk calf stood at the edge of the woods, gazing at the meadow beyond, searching for her herd. It was September, and the elk's mating season, also known as rut, had just begun. The bulls were fighting over the females, and their loud bugling could be heard throughout the wilderness of northeastern Oregon. Most of the battles involved little more than a show of force, but sometimes the male elk went after each other, stabbing and pushing with their huge racks of antlers until the weaker bull gave up and ran away. The winner then gathered his harem, or group of females, to breed with. After rut, the males left the harem to be alone or they found other bulls and formed small groups. The females stayed together throughout the year.

Frightened by the battling bulls, the young elk had run off, losing track of her mother and the other females in her group. Now she was desperate to return to them. She weighed about two hundred pounds, half

Yellowstone Park's Druid Peak pack after a bull elk. Chances are, the elk got away. Studies have shown that wolves are successful in their hunts less than twenty percent of the time.

the size she would be as an adult. Like the six-month-old wolf pups of the Imnaha pack, this would be her first winter, and her hair had grown thick to keep her warm. The spots she'd been born with had nearly disappeared. Her tail and the area around it were light in color compared to the reddish-brown of the rest of her coat. The word *wapiti*, which is another name for elk, comes from the Shawnee and Cree word *waapitit*, meaning "white rump."

Nearby, Sophie and the gray pup had wandered away from the rest of the pack, intent on finding food. Sophie picked up the young elk's scent and followed it until she and the pup stood a few yards away from the frightened animal. Predator and prey exchanged a quick glance, and then the elk bolted. Sophie took chase. The pup gathered his long legs beneath him and followed. Sophie was a fast and experienced hunter, and her son struggled to keep up with her, maneuvering around clumps of grass too tall to see over and leaping over a wide stream. He had watched from the sidelines as his parents had brought down deer, and he'd played hard at hunting games with his siblings, but this was the real thing, and the gray pup felt the excitement of the hunt as the three animals, all intent on their own survival, bounded silently across the meadow.*

Closer and closer the wolves came, with Sophie a few feet in front of her pup. He could hear the elk's rapid breaths and smell the warm

* *The 330,000-acre Zumwalt Prairie in northeastern Oregon is one of the largest remaining natural prairies in the world. This prairie runs along the western edge of Hells Canyon and is home to a variety of wildlife, including raptors and many other birds, black bears, deer, elk, and once again, wolves.*

scent of her. Chunks of dirt flung from her flying hooves hit his face. Suddenly, Sophie leapt, her body propelled forward, and her teeth sank into the white hindquarters of the elk. The calf stumbled and the wolf pup jumped, throwing himself at her. But rather than getting a taste of elk, he found himself tumbling in the grass with Sophie beside him. He had made contact with the calf, but at the same time, he'd collided with his mother, causing her to lose her grip on the elk. The calf took off with a fresh burst of speed, and the distance between them grew. The pup whined, wanting to continue the hunt, but his mother stood still as she watched the elk flee across the meadow and into the forest. Sophie knew this was a meal they would never catch.

DARTED!

February 25, 2011, was a cold day in northeastern Oregon. The temperature was well below zero when Roblyn and Russ jumped into a helicopter to search for wolves. Their pilot kept the helicopter low, while a small airplane, called a spotter plane, flew overhead. With the heat cranked high inside the cabin, the biologist in the spotter plane searched the rugged Oregon wilderness for wolves on the snow-covered ground. Finally, he

Pups from the Imnaha pack, approximately 2.5 months old, captured by remote camera.

PHOTO: ODFW REMOTE CAMERA, JULY 7, 2013.

Roblyn and Russ put a new collar on OR-4, father of OR-7.

saw a pair running below, their gray bodies moving quickly over the snow, and he radioed the helicopter pilot. Roblyn and Russ studied the wolves through the open doorway of the helicopter as the spinning blades of the propeller brought the machine closer to the fleeing animals. This wasn't OR-2 or her mate, OR-4, but since they were in the territory of the Imnaha pack, the biologists knew the running wolves must be two of their pups. The pups would be ten months old this time of year and nearly the size of adults.

The helicopter flew low, and Russ, tied in with a safety harness, leaned out the doorway and aimed his tranquilizer gun at the fleeing wolves. He fired, and the dart hit the hip of the young male. The surprised animal kept running and the spotter plane followed it as the helicopter chased the other wolf. Russ aimed and fired and darted that one as well. The wolves ran for a short distance and then slowed to a trot, followed by a wobbly walk. Within a few minutes, both dropped to the ground as if in a deep sleep.

The helicopter landed and Russ jumped out to collar the male wolf. Roblyn was in charge of the second one, a gray female. Working in the bitter cold wasn't easy, and the two biologists had a lot to do. They took blood samples of the unconscious animals, measured and weighed them, then placed a 1½-pound collar around each wolf's neck. By the time everything was done, the tranquilized wolves were waking up. Russ and Roblyn watched them struggle to stand on shaky legs and then trot slowly away, then the biologists climbed back into the helicopter to return to the warmth of their office.

The ninety-pound male wolf they had just handled was given the title of OR-7, the seventh wolf collared in the state of Oregon. The female was named OR-8. No photos were taken that day. It was simply too cold. Besides, Roblyn and Russ had no idea that the young male, now known as OR-7, would someday become one of the most famous wolves in the world.

BACK TO THE PACK

OR-7 didn't know why his hip was sore. And he didn't understand why there was a heavy band around his neck. All his shaking did nothing to set him free from the collar. He hurried away from the noise of the strange thing that flew in the sky, wanting to put as much distance as he could between himself and the noise of the helicopter, as well as the two-legged creatures that had stood above him when he awoke.

His sister had been with him, but she was nowhere in sight. He stopped to listen and catch a whiff of her. With a sense of smell a hundred times that of a human's, the young wolf could easily detect odors. But the scent of his sister was gone. He was alone in the forest, far from family or familiar ground. He broke into a run,

PHOTO: ODFW TRAIL CAMERA DECEMBER 14, 2012.

This wolf family, known as the Minam pack, lives in the Eagle Cap Wilderness of northeastern Oregon.

tail tucked between his legs. Running was not easy. The drug from the tranquilizer dart was still working its way through his body. His legs went in different directions and he nearly fell. When his head cleared and he found his stride, OR-7 ran for a long time, until he heard the distant sound of his mother's howl. He turned and went toward her, over boulders and thick brush, down the side of one mountain and up another. Finally, he was reunited with his pack. He lay belly up on the ground as his mother nudged him with her nose, smelling the thing around his neck. The other wolves gathered too, sniffing him thoroughly. OR-7 whined and licked the muzzles of the curious wolves, relieved to be in the safety of the pack. Life was back to normal, yet he would always know the fear created by the loud, whirling bird in the sky and, even more, the fear of the humans who had brought all this about.

FAMILY LIFE

Wolf families differ as much as human ones do. Some have only a few members, while others have many. The overall average is from four to seven animals. One of the largest known groups of gray wolves was the Druid Peak pack in Yellowstone National Park, which in the year

Yellowstone's former Druid Peak pack.

PHOTO: DAN STAHLER, NATIONAL PARK SERVICE.

2001 reached a high of thirty-seven animals! But life is difficult for wild wolves, and the Druid Peak pack lost members because of starvation and from fights with other packs. Some left to join other family groups. Also, hunters shot several of the wolves when they left the safety of the park. Fifteen years later, the largest known pack had only one remaining member. When she died, the Druid Peak pack was gone.

The makeup of the wolves in a group varies as well. There is usually one male and female pair that breeds in late winter and has pups in the spring, although other members may reproduce too. The offspring from previous litters may remain in the pack, playing important roles in babysitting and educating new pups when they arrive.* Sometimes, wolves travel and start new packs, which helps to keep the gene pool diverse. This is known as dispersal and occurs most commonly when wolves are still young, often only one or two years old.

Wolves that leave the safety of their families are at higher risk of going hungry or being attacked by other animals, including territorial wolves from other packs. We know little about what prompts certain wolves to leave while others stay. Perhaps it is because they are not comfortable with the position they hold in their pack. Perhaps they leave because eventually there wouldn't be enough food to go around if all of them stayed. For whatever reason, dispersal is common among wolves, and it serves to spread their species throughout the land, including to places where their populations were previously destroyed by humans.

* You may have heard of the term "alpha" used for the breeding pair in a wolf pack. This term originated in the 1930s and 1940s as a scientist named Rudolph Schenkel studied wolves in Switzerland's Basel Zoo. Schenkel's work was important and taught people a great deal about wolves, but it led us to believe wolves were very competitive, always striving to become the "top dog." Although some wolves are certainly more dominant than others, we have come to recognize the flexibility of wolf societies and how they communicate with each other and work together as a unit.

CHAPTER THREE

The Journey Begins

The crisp, golden leaves of the cottonwood trees rustled in the breeze. OR-7 lifted his muzzle to catch the scents coming downwind. He took in a hint of elk, but from far away. There was a feline smell, cougar or bobcat, also from far away. He found nothing in the air to concern him, and he wasn't hungry, so there was no need to hunt. The afternoon sun warmed the assortment of gray, brown, and black guard hairs on his back. His dense, soft undercoat was growing thick in preparation for the cold weather to come. This would be his second winter.

The young wolf turned to look at the members of his pack, who were resting in a clearing a few yards away. They were soaking up the fall sunshine, their bellies full from a recent meal of mule deer. Sophie slept soundly, while OR-4 sat on a large boulder overlooking the valley below. Two of OR-7's siblings quarreled over a piece of hide. This was a peaceful time for the wolves. The flies and mosquitoes that had been so pesky all summer had died in the recent frost. Prey was plentiful and the winter's chill and heavy snow had yet to arrive.

OR-7 returned his gaze to the horizon. There was nothing he saw or heard or smelled to draw him away from the security of his pack and the familiar surroundings of home. But something beckoned him, something instinctual that had spoken to wolves for thousands and thousands of years. This voice told him it was time to strike out on his own. "For the

* From the poem *The Law for the Wolves* by Rudyard Kipling. See page 63.

strength of the pack is the wolf, and the strength of the wolf is the pack,"* but OR-7 would soon be a lone wolf facing danger each day without the help of his family. He stood, shook himself, sending dirt and bits of leaves flying. Then he trotted off, moving in a southern direction. He did not look back. His long journey had begun.

MOVING ON

OR-7's radio collar relayed readings of his location to the computers at the Oregon Department of Fish and Wildlife. Roblyn and Russ watched and recorded his travels but didn't think much of it, even when the young wolf had gone more than one hundred miles. They had noticed that often wolves would go on a pre-dispersal trip, in which they left for a time, then returned to their pack before embarking on a longer journey. Besides, they had plenty of wolves to watch over. There were at least twenty-three of them living in the wilds of Oregon, and several of these animals wore collars as well.

After leaving his family on September 10, 2011, OR-7 traveled south from his homeland, trotting across private property, then entering large, isolated tracts of public lands. Public lands are managed by government agencies but belong to the American people. Within some public lands are roadless areas, lands managed by the National Forest Service or Bureau of Land Management where road building is restricted. Limiting road construction ensures that we have plac-

PHOTO: ODFW, MAY 3, 2009.

The first radio-collared wolf in Oregon.

es in the environment that are free of the noise and destruction caused by vehicles. These quiet places are used by people for hiking and other forms of outdoor recreation. Roadless areas also allow wild animals to disperse across vast areas without the risk of being hit by cars.

View of Mt. Thielsen from Umpqua National Forest.

Wildlife corridors likewise provide safe routes for traveling animals. These corridors link areas, some of them across great distances of land, so wildlife can move naturally. An example of this is the 120-mile trip taken each year by a herd of three hundred pronghorn antelope. These antelope migrate as they have for six thousand years, from Grand Teton National Park in northwestern Wyoming south to the Upper Green Valley, also in Wyoming. Development is prohibited on this pathway to ensure the safety of the antelope.

Late autumn of 2011, six weeks after OR-7 had dispersed, Roblyn and Russ checked the computer program that was tracking the young wolf and discovered that he had traveled more than 250 miles, skirting towns and crossing highways to trot over the crest of the Cascade mountain range into the Umpqua National Forest. Now he had their attention. OR-7 had just become the first wild wolf in Western Oregon in sixty-five years. There was a good chance he walked right by the site where the last known wolf in the area was killed and turned in for a $5 bounty in 1946.

Russ and Roblyn shared the news of OR-7's achievement with the media, and the word spread in newspapers and on television stations across the United States and to other countries. People from around the

The first photo of OR-7 was captured on November 14, 2011, by a trail camera belonging to Allen Daniels.

world were excited to know that this one lone wolf had ventured into territory where *Canis lupus* had not lived in decades. OR-7 became famous overnight.

FIRST PHOTO

Near the tiny Southern Oregon logging town of Butte Falls, a hunter set up a trail camera deep in the forest, hoping to catch pictures of deer. Trail cameras are portable devices that take pictures automatically when something moves in front of them. Usually, the wild animal has no idea the cameras are there because they are well hidden and take pictures without making a sound. Our traveling wolf paused right in front of the deer hunter's camera, as if he were posing for his picture. When the photo was released, people were thrilled to see what the mystery wolf looked like. Although the picture was a grainy black-and-white, it showed OR-7's steel-gray coloring and the dark band down his shoulder blades formed by a pattern of black hairs. His legs were tan-colored and long. His face had the typical mask of most wolves. OR-7's nose was on the ground, probably sniffing around for a snack. He was indeed a handsome wolf.

Oregon Wild is a non-profit organization that works hard to support the environment. They educate people about wolves and campaign widely to protect them. In January 2012, Oregon Wild sponsored a naming contest for OR-7. A previous competition they hosted had given OR-2 the nickname of Sophie. The staff at Oregon Wild hoped this new contest would draw attention to OR-7's story and would help publicize wolf recovery in our country. Also, the Oregon Wild staff believed that if OR-7 became better known, he was less likely to be shot. So a competition was launched to give the young wolf a more personal name, one fitting for the celebrity he had become. Children from all over the globe, including Finland and Nigeria, sent in ideas for names. One entry from a thirteen-year-old in Eastern Oregon suggested the name Lupin. Another came from a boy in Oklahoma who liked the name Takota, which means "friend" in Shoshone. Two girls, a seven-year-old from Idaho and an eleven-year-old from North Dakota, both came up with the same suggestion. Their entry was chosen as the winner, and OR-7 became known as Journey, a name that fit him well.

Journey's story continued to spread across the world through newspapers, television, and the Internet. He was featured in *The New York Times*, *National Geographic*, and on the British Broadcasting Corporation. People in China and Japan knew about him, as did folks in Brazil and Africa. Why were people so drawn to this one lone wolf? Perhaps they saw Journey as an adventurer who liked to travel to new and exciting places. Perhaps they thought of Journey as an animal struggling to survive against all odds. Wolves are pack animals that hunt together, raise pups as a family, and enjoy playing with each other, but Journey was by himself, struggling to find food and stay alive. People cheered for him from the sidelines, hoping that each day he would find a bite to eat and stay away from cars and other dangers, such as traps and guns. Journey became an inspiration to us all.

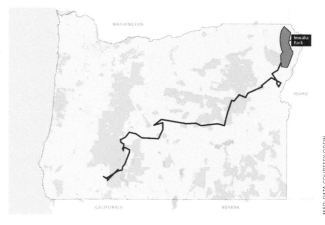

MAP: DATA COURTESY ODFW.

Dispersal of OR-7 from Imnaha Wolf Pack, September 10 – November 19, 2011. This map from shows how far Journey traveled in just over two months.

AT THE LAKE

Journey was hungry again. Wolves can "wolf down" more than twenty pounds of meat at a sitting, but it had been months since he had been that full. Bringing down an elk or a deer by himself had proven to be not only difficult but dangerous as well. He'd learned early on that the sharp hooves and antlers of the animals they hunt could injure wolves.

The young wolf ambled across the snow-covered ground, heading southward. He had not heard the sound of car engines, slamming doors, or human voices for a long time. He relaxed, moving forward at a steady six miles an hour. He ascended a ridge and then stopped at the top. Below him appeared a large, round lake with a small island off the edge of the shore. Its surface was as clear as a mirror and a deep, dark blue. Journey headed down the steep embankment toward the lake, sliding on the loose rocks and dirt. He smelled humans, but saw and heard none. The edge of the lake was frozen. He stepped on it carefully, testing the ice. Beneath him, bubbles appeared. With his broad feet, Journey pawed at the bubbles, and a thin sheet of ice broke loose. He grabbed the ice with his teeth and crunched, feeling the coldness. Then he hopped up and down with both front paws pounding the frozen water until another piece broke loose. He picked up this section with his mouth and shook it as though it were an animal he was trying to kill.

Journey played at the edge of the lake for a long time before he continued on. Although he didn't realize it, he had spent the evening at Crater Lake National Park, a favorite spot for people to visit in Oregon. This lake was formed more than five thousand years ago when a volcanic mountain named Mount Mazama erupted and collapsed in on itself, creating a caldera that eventually became Crater Lake, the deepest lake in the United States and the ninth deepest in the world.

Journey rose early the next morning. The snow was crusty and cold, but he trotted over it easily, his

Crater Lake National Park.

broad, furry feet working like snowshoes over the winter landscape. Suddenly, he stopped. The breeze carried to him a delicious scent. Journey changed directions and hurried toward the smell. He had eaten only a few mice over the last several days, not enough to fill up a ninety-pound wolf, and the anticipation of a hearty meal made his stomach growl.

Journey loped across an open field, his long legs moving effortlessly. In the center of the field, he discovered the body of an elk calf. The young elk had caught its legs in a wire fence a few days before. A man driving by had seen the animal struggling to escape and stopped to release it. Despite the man's help, the calf had been badly injured and soon died. This meant Journey had a hearty meal. The hungry wolf fed on the carcass, tearing away the tough skin to expose the soft flesh beneath. He paused when he heard the sound of a vehicle approaching on a nearby road. Grabbing a mouthful of meat, he left the carcass and disappeared into a gully lined with willow trees. He waited there until the sound went away and then returned to feed some more. Journey stayed in the area for several days, eating and resting. It was good to be full.

HOWLING PARTY

Eighteen miles south of Crater Lake is a cozy place to stay called the Crystalwood Lodge, owned by Liz Parrish. Besides running the lodge, Liz is a dog musher who trains and cares for over twenty sled dogs. In 2008, the year she turned fifty, Liz raced in the Iditarod, a thousand-mile dog sled race held every year in Alaska. Standing only five feet tall, she was known as Iditarod's "Littlest Musher." Participating in this race was a dream come true for Liz, but traveling across the frozen ground in the far reaches of Alaska was not

Liz Parrish at the 2008 Iditarod.

an easy task. It took her two weeks to finish. She had to stay warm on be-low-zero nights, feed her dogs, and keep them warm as well. And Liz was always on the lookout for moose, huge animals that stand six feet tall and weigh more than eight hundred pounds. Moose can be dangerous to sled dog teams, attacking and stomping on the dogs if they invade their habitat.

It was a sunny November afternoon in 2011 when Liz jumped in her truck to drive into town for supplies. At the end of her long driveway, she came to a sudden stop. Beneath a fifty-foot cedar tree stood an animal Liz knew was a wolf. It was much larger than her dogs, gray in color, long-legged with oversized feet. You must be Journey, she thought, the wolf I've heard so much about. Liz sat in her truck and stared. Journey stood still and watched her as well, his gaze locked as though trying to figure out what Liz intended to do about him standing on her property. Liz had seen wolves in the wild in Alaska and while training her dogs in Minnesota. She knew there was no reason to be afraid. In fact, she was thrilled. Journey, the famous lone wolf, was posed beneath her tree as if he belonged there.

"I was stunned—it was such a huge animal," Liz told reporters. "He just stopped and stared. I stopped and stared. We had a stare down that seemed like a long time, but was probably just a few seconds."

Liz glanced down at the seat beside her to see if her camera was there so she could snap a picture of Journey. But when she looked back up, he was gone, evaporated into the trees as if he were a ghost.

A few days later, Liz heard her sled dogs howling. She had just fed them, and they often sang after dinner, as if thanking her for their meal. But this time the dogs' howls were answered by a deep, low voice. Liz knew she was hearing the call of OR-7. She searched for him for days but did not see him again. The wandering wolf had stopped only briefly before continuing his travels south. He had journeyed over seven hundred miles in his long search for a new home.*

*"Some minutes later, from ten miles away on the towering black-timbered shoulders of Pole Mountain, there stole out the most desolate cry in all the world—the howl of the grey timber wolf. It rode on the upper air without a tremor, high and thin, pointed as a needle. Through long minutes the note was sustained, mournful and remote—through long moments it died, with a falling cadence of profound listlessness; and even before it ceased, it had become the very essence of the quiet of the night." From *My Friend Flicka*, by Mary O'Hara.

THE GOLDEN STATE

Journey's travels took him to the southern edge of Oregon and across a trail known as the Pacific Crest Trail, or PCT. This path begins in Mexico and continues through California, Oregon, and Washington. After 2,650 long miles, the PCT ends in Canada. Strong-willed hikers travel the trail, sometimes for the entire distance, often for shorter hikes. To hike the entire PCT takes three to four months and several pairs of good hiking shoes.

A favorite stop for hikers on the PCT is Little Hyatt Lake in Southern Oregon. This small lake is home to otters, ducks, and geese, as well as other animals. Cattails grow at one end of the lake, while a narrow dam creates a waterfall at the other end. Along the banks are soft places to lay a sleeping bag and good spots to throw in a fishing line.

PHOTO: BOB WICK, BUREAU OF LAND MANAGEMENT.

Views from the Pacific Crest Trail where it meanders through the Cascade-Siskiyou National Monument in Southern Oregon.

Trails for humans are trails for animals too. One morning, a woman hiking the PCT near Little Hyatt Lake came over the hill below the lake to see Journey trotting along the shore. She had been following the adventures of the lone wolf in the newspaper and knew right away who he was. Later that day, she had lunch at a local café and shared her story with people there. Seeing a wolf in the wild is an experience most of us never forget.

It was just after Christmas. Journey had left behind the tranquil setting of Little Hyatt Lake. He was still traveling south, still in search of a mate and a territory to call his own. Wolves know nothing of state lines, of breaking records, or of becoming famous, but on December 28, 2011, Journey crossed the border from Oregon into California, making history again, this time for becoming the first wild wolf in the state of California in nearly a century.

People across the world, including Amaroq Weiss, were thrilled when Journey entered California. In her words, "On December 28th a young male wolf known as OR-7 (aka Journey) lifted a paw on the Oregon side of the border and set it back down in California. In that moment, he became the first wild wolf confirmed in our state in 87 years, signaling the return of a species we once drove to extinction. For Californians, this wolf's journey is our journey. His howl ringing out in the cold mountain air is our own howl of joy at his presence."

As with nearly everywhere in the United States, wolves had once been common in California. But people had driven them out, afraid the predator would kill their cattle or eat too many elk and deer. The last wild wolf in California died in 1924 after being caught in a trap. This wolf was a tough one. He had already lost one leg to a trap before he was caught again, this time for the last time.

Journey came into California at the edge of the Lower Klamath National Wildlife Refuge. Flat acres of shallow water can be seen in all directions at this refuge. Bald eagles and hawks perch in the trees, their sharp eyes watchful for prey. Geese, ducks, egrets, cranes, pelicans, and other waterfowl fly over Klamath Lake and land on its sparkling waters. Each species makes a distinctive sound, filling the air with their honks and chirps and quacks. This is a wonderful place for birds, but not a place a wolf would want to call home. Journey found a spot where the land divided the water and trotted deeper into California, heading for drier ground.

PHOTO: US FISH AND WILDLIFE SERVICE.

Pintail ducks at the Lower Klamath National Wildlife Refuge.

The California Department of Fish and Wildlife kept track of OR-7 now, receiving information from his GPS collar. They created a website about him. They even started a Twitter account for the popular wolf. The department gave the public a general idea of where Journey was, but they did not give out exact details about his location. Some people still don't believe wolves have a right to exist, so every effort was made to keep Journey safe.

🐾 🐾 JOURNEY FINDS SOME FRIENDS

He had been away from home for a long, long time. It was early spring and the days were getting longer in Modoc County, a remote area of Northern California. The sun was scorching and the ground bone dry from lack of rain. Journey continued his search for a mate. He stopped frequently to urinate on trees, brushes, and rocks, leaving his own personal scent mark. He came back to these sites frequently, checking with his nose to determine if another wolf had left its mark over his. But none did, and when he howled, no wolf returned his call.*

One morning, Journey heard a sound that woke him from a deep sleep. He jumped up and cocked his head to listen. It was a howl, but not the howl of wolves. The sound reached a high note and then quivered and became a series of loud yelps. Journey didn't care if these weren't wolves, he wanted some company. He trotted to the source of the sound and discovered three coyotes ambling along the side of a hill. The coyotes caught Journey's scent and stopped, staring at the wolf from the hillside.

Journey walked with raised hackles and a stiff gait toward the coyotes. The smaller one darted off, tail between its legs, but the other two held their ground. Journey came closer. Soon, he was within a foot of

* Much of the mileage OR-7 traveled in California was made while going from one scent post to another, over and over again. GPS maps created of his wanderings looked at times like a gnarled ball of yarn, with strands going out in all directions. We assume that Journey returned to his scent posts so frequently in order to see if another wolf had marked over his scent. Wolves communicate in many intricate ways, and scent is a primary one.

them. They all shared the same grayish coat color, but Journey stood about ten inches taller than the coyotes and was nearly fifty pounds heavier. When their snouts met for a sniff, Journey's was much broader and his ears more rounded. He turned to the tail end of the coyotes and smelled there. They did the same to him. The third coyote, curiosity overriding fear, crept up to the group to join in the sniffing. His tail wagged and he licked the chin of the wolf, but Journey met this friendliness with a deep growl. Satisfied with the introductions, Journey moved away from the group. The coyotes followed, keeping a respectable distance from their larger cousin as they worked their way across the hillside together.

In a place where wolves and coyotes exist together, coyotes see wolves as a threat and do their best to stay away from them. Perhaps the coyotes had forgotten this lesson, as it had been many generations since wolves had inhabited their territory. Perhaps Journey had forgotten as well, or maybe he just wanted to be near other animals similar to himself.*

PHOTO: NPS.

* *Like wolves, coyotes play an essential role in the environment. They control rodent populations, helping to reduce the spread of diseases carried by rodents. Coyotes also clean up their surroundings by eating carrion. Despite the benefit of these small canines, they are the frequent target of poisoning, trapping, and shooting. Research has found that randomly killing coyotes causes an increase in their population, rather than a decrease. When adult coyotes are killed, their pack dynamics are disrupted, resulting in more breeding by younger members of the family group. Also, the loss of mature adults means there is no one to teach the young to hunt, so they resort to easier prey, such as livestock. The same is thought to be true of wolf populations.*

SECOND PHOTO

Journey was known as the ghost wolf to the California Department of Fish and Wildlife. Although the department's computers identified the wolf's location several times a day, whenever the staff drove out to find him, OR-7 was nowhere to be seen.

But on a bright May morning in 2012, biologist Richard Shinn and other members of the department were in the right place at the right time. GPS signals had told them that Journey was close to some ranches in Modoc County, so Richard and the others headed out to let the livestock owners know the wolf was nearby. Making the ranchers aware of Journey's general location allowed them to watch their livestock closely so problems with the wolf could be avoided.

The group drove to the vicinity of the ranches, got out of their truck, and stood together, surrounded by the open terrain of far Northern California. Richard scanned his binoculars across a sagebrush-covered hillside, and in the frame of his lens, he saw OR-7, the elusive gray wolf, looking right back at him from a distance of about a hundred yards. The ghost wolf sighted at last! Journey moved away and two coyotes joined him, walking close to the wolf. Richard grabbed his camera and snapped the second picture taken of OR-7, this one in color, as the wolf edged his way along the side of the hill amidst the pale green of the sagebrush.

Journey in a sagebrush hillside in Modoc County, California.

ANNIVERSARY

December 28, 2012, marked the one-year anniversary of Journey's move to California. He traveled across the sparsely populated northern part of the state, spending time near Lake Almanor and Lava Beds National Monument. He headed east, over Wolf Creek, named for his ancestors that once lived here, to the Sierra Nevada mountain range, where he came close to entering Nevada. Journey's search for a mate was a lonely

PHOTO: ODFW.

* Fladry comes from the German word *flattern*, which means "to flutter." The Wood River Project, initiated by Defenders of Wildlife in 2007, has nearly eliminated sheep losses in the Wood River Valley of Idaho by using non-lethal measures including fladry, guard dogs and increased human presence.

one, with little chance for success. He could not have known that wolves hadn't inhabited this area for nearly one hundred years.

Some livestock owners in the state expressed concern that if wolves returned, their livestock would be in danger. This is a legitimate concern, as ranchers and farmers depend on their animals for their livelihood, and wolves do occasionally prey on sheep and cattle. But there are effective ways to help protect livestock from wolves. One of the first things ranchers do is remove bone piles, a sort of graveyard for dead livestock, but without the burial. Wolves come to these bone piles to feed on the carcasses. In fact, Journey visited several on his trip to California. The problem with allowing wolves at bone piles is that this brings them in close proximity to livestock operations, and the closer wolves are to domestic animals, the more chances for depredations to occur.

Ranchers also use fladry to protect their animals. Fladry is a line of red or orange flag-like strips secured to fences that contain livestock. Centuries ago, fladry was used in Russia and Eastern Europe as a way of catching wolves. Hunters chased wild wolves into an enclosure created by the waving flags. Once inside, the wolves would not cross the barrier and were easily shot by the hunters. Today, fladry is used to keep wolves out. Wolves are naturally shy and suspicious, and the waving strips keep them away, at least for a while. This technique works best in smaller pastures and pens. Sometimes, the fladry is used along with an electric wire. This is called turbo-fladry.*

The use of guard dogs is also an ancient practice and still an effective one. Large breeds like the Great Pyrenees, Maremma, Akbash, and others are trained to live with livestock, especially sheep, and protect them from predators. If a wolf wanders near the flock, the dogs warn their humans with loud barks. They will even stand up to a wolf to protect their sheep. However, no dog is a match for *Canis lupus*, especially a pack of them, and livestock guardian dogs have lost these battles more than once.

Another tactic to keep livestock safe is for sheepherders and cattle owners to spend more time with their animals on the open range. Some use range riders who travel on horseback or four-wheelers to monitor the livestock and keep a look out for wolves. Their presence alone will often scare hungry predators away.

It takes a creative livestock owner to stay on top of the hungry and resourceful wolf. The rancher must change his or her techniques once the predator becomes accustomed to them. And each ranch or farm is unique; what works to prevent problems in one location may not work for the neighbor down the road. But with ingenuity and patience, as well as an understanding of predator behavior, livestock owners around the world are finding ways to coexist with wolves.

This picture shows a range rider working in northeastern Oregon.

PHOTO: DIANE HUNTER, COURTESY OF ODFW.

Journey's Wandering
Path through California

December 2011 – December 2012

January 2013

February 2013

March 2013

April 2013

MAP: DATA COURTESY OF CALIFORNIA DEPARTMENT OF FISH AND WILDLIFE.

CHAPTER FOUR

Settling In

Some thought he would stay in California forever, but in early spring of 2013, Journey headed north back into Oregon. He crossed the border near the old mining town of Yreka, California, dodging cars as he trotted across busy Interstate 5 before moving northeast into the Rogue River-Siskiyou National Forest.

Shortly after OR-7 returned to his home state, Mark Vargas, an Oregon Department of Fish and Wildlife biologist, and his daughter, Jennifer, did their best to get some pictures of the elusive wolf. It was early April in 2013, on the annual Take Your Daughter to Work Day. This event is an opportunity for girls to see in person what their parents do at their jobs.

Jennifer, a sixteen-year-old high school student, was glad to have this time with her dad. They drove together deep into the Rogue River-Siskiyou National Forest. The narrow road was lined with fifty-foot ponderosa pines. With an elevation of nearly five thousand feet, patches of snowfall still clung to the ground. In the shaded forest, the snow was still deep. Jennifer and Mark peered into the open spaces between the tree trunks, searching for Journey. They had more than their eyes to help them find the wolf. A week before, Mark had driven to the area and strapped a trail camera to a tree near where Journey had been feeding on an elk carcass. As the wolf's GPS collar transmitted signals, location information was displayed on the computer in Mark's office, telling him exactly where Journey was.

When Mark and Jennifer neared the elk carcass, they parked and got out of the truck. Mark pulled a metal pole device from the back of the pickup. What looked like an old-fashioned television antenna that people once put on the roofs of their homes was actually a VHF antenna. VHF devices pick up signals from collared wildlife when the animal is nearby.

They walked down the narrow logging road together, Mark carrying the VHF antenna and listening for a signal telling him the wolf was close. The ground was covered in wildlife footprints. The feet of a coyote had left tracks much like a wolf's but smaller. Ravens had walked in the snow, leaving their splayfooted prints. And there were also big, round cat tracks, nearly five inches wide. Cougar.

Jennifer and Mark followed the cougar tracks into the woods and stopped at a small clearing. The snow was gone there and the white rib cage of the elk lay on the ground, picked clean of meat. A femur bone, chewed in half, was nearly hidden by fallen leaves. The elk's skull lay on the ground a few feet away, with a large hole in the top portion. The skull was almost a foot long, with the teeth still intact. The eye sockets were round holes the size of silver dollars.

Mark walked to the trail camera. The display screen told him that nine minutes of video had been shot. He removed the camera and walked back to the truck, where he took the memory card out and plugged it into his laptop to upload the short videos. One clip showed him setting up and walking away from the camera the previous week. The next showed Mark and Jennifer approaching. But that was it. No cougar, no ravens, and more importantly, no wolf. Nothing. Something had malfunctioned, or the camera had not been programmed correctly. Either way, Journey had escaped the curiosity of humans once again. Mark and Jennifer drove off, disappointed, but feeling fortunate to have been so close to the famous wolf.

PHOTO: ODFW, 2007.

My, what big feet you have!

NO LONGER A LONE WOLF

The lean, black wolf wandered into eastern Jackson County of southwestern Oregon. She had been on her own for several months now, having left her home and her pack to travel west of the Cascade Range in search of a mate.

It was midwinter and snow covered the ground. Soon it would be February and the time when the black wolf would be ready to reproduce. The nearing of this time caused her to step up her search for a mate. She squatted often, marking bushes and clumps of grass with her urine. She searched the air for the scent of another wolf. She howled, then sat down and listened for a response. With eyes that could catch movement from miles away, the black wolf stood on the top of ridges and searched the wooded areas and meadows of the Rogue River-Siskiyou National Forest.

A few miles away, Journey was doing the same thing. He had picked up an enticing new scent. Although he hadn't eaten much in the last few days, he ignored the rumbling of his stomach and headed in the direction the scent led him, marking trees and shrubs along the way.

Journey and the black wolf met where the edge of the forest joined a wide-open field. She hung back in the woods at first, knowing that being a new wolf in the territory of another could lead to a fight. Her form was barely visible in the dark shadows of the trees, but Journey could see her and he hurried forward. The long guard hairs on his back stood up, giving him the appearance of being a larger wolf than he was. He held his tail high and moved with a stiff gait. It had been a long, long time since he'd been in the presence of another wolf.

She broke from the woods and ran into the thick grass of the meadow. Journey pursued. The female ran with tail tucked, taking quick glances behind to see how close her pursuer was. This slowed her long enough for OR-7 to catch up. His body met the black wolf's and she tumbled, and then lay in the grass, belly up and feet pawing the air. Journey stood over her and pushed his nose into her fur, pulling in her scent. She whined, and the tip of his tail wagged.

The black wolf began to rise, but Journey growled so she rolled to her side, raising her head to watch the other wolf. He sat down a few feet from her, taking in the sight and scent of her with the backdrop of the forest behind. They stayed like that for several minutes until the female stood and approached him, tail low and wagging. She extended her tongue and licked his muzzle, whining. Journey rose, and the pair moved together along the bank of the creek. They trotted side by side with shoulders touching, tails wagging, and tongues darting out to give frequent wolf kisses. After three long years alone, Journey had found a mate.

PHOTO: US FISH AND WILDLIFE SERVICE TRAIL CAMERA, MAY 14, 2014.

A trail camera set by the US Fish and Wildlife Service captured this image of the mysterious black wolf on May 14, 2014.

MYSTERY SOLVED

March 2014. Journey had stopped wandering. When biologists, including Russ and Roblyn, along with John Stephenson of the US Fish and Wildlife Service, noticed the change in the wolf's GPS readings, they became suspicious. Early spring was the time for wolves to breed and prepare for pups. But it takes more than one wolf to create a family. John and his associates traveled into the Rogue River-Siskiyou National Forest. Trail cameras were set up. There was little to do now but wait.

Two months later, their suspicions were confirmed. Photos taken by the trail camera showed not only OR-7, but a black wolf as well. The black wolf was smaller than Journey, with a slender head. And she squatted to urinate, providing proof that she was a she. The black female had found him, or he had found her. However it happened, Journey was no longer alone.

Although far from glamorous, one of the most important jobs in the world of wolf research is the study of scat, the term used for wild animal feces. When the black wolf was seen in the trail camera photos, the next step was to find samples of her scat. Much can be learned about the animal from its feces. By the size, shape, color, and makeup of the scat, one can identify what type of animal left it. With some dissection of the sample (please, use a stick!), it may become apparent what the animal ate. A sliver of deer hoof, the beak of a small bird, bone fragments, and other body parts are frequently found. Bears leave a lot of berries in their scat. The hair of the animal eaten is often visible. Grass and other vegetation may be seen, sometimes the result of an effort to purge an upset tummy.

But the finer details of the secrets contained in scat comes from DNA studies done in a laboratory. Once the black wolf's scat was found, the sample was sent to the University of Idaho. There, her DNA was compared to previous findings from other wolf scat collected in northeastern Oregon. Eventually, a report was released. Journey's mate was from the Minam and Snake River packs, neighbors to the Imnaha pack. She had made the same long trip as Journey, but as she did not wear a collar, no one had known.*

NEW LIFE IN THE FOREST

The black wolf dug into the dark earth. She'd chosen this site for her den because it was sheltered on one side by a long-ago fallen pine tree. And,

* We all know how dogs love to sniff poop. As a way of putting this behavior to good use, both purebreds and shelter dogs are being trained to find scat. A trained dog alerts its handler each time it discovers a sample and is then rewarded with play or a treat. The goal may be to determine the population numbers of an endangered species or to see how a species is affected by humans or other animals. Dogs are able to sniff out scat from a species as small as a caterpillar!

with the help of rain, wind, and snow, the dead tree was breaking down. Its bark and trunk and pine needles slowly joined the earth, making for soft soil and easy digging. She worked without pause, her front paws moving in a rapid cycling motion. The dirt flew beneath her belly and behind her back legs, forming a mound on the forest floor.

Journey sat in the shade watching, head cocked to one side, intrigued with the black wolf's activities. Finally, he stood and joined her and the pair dug side by side to create a home for their soon-to-be-born pups. Instinctually, the wolves knew the den would be a safer place if it were large enough for the pups and the mother to hide in, out of sight of other wild creatures that might bring harm to the newborn litter. With the efforts of the wolves' four paws, the hole grew quickly and was soon more than three feet deep and two feet wide, angling in one direction to form a tunnel.

A long-tailed, olive-colored squirrel chattered from a nearby stump. Journey stopped digging and took chase, deciding a late-morning snack would taste good. The squirrel leapt onto the trunk of a tall madrone tree and scrambled to the top, leaving Journey staring up from the bottom. The squirrel had outsmarted him, so he trotted off in search of easier prey.

The black wolf felt no desire to eat. It was the middle of April and her belly was heavy with pups. If she lived in a more northern latitude like Alaska, it would be May before her pups were due, but in Southern Oregon, this was the time for wolves to deliver their young. She spent several minutes widening the end of the tunnel so it was large enough for her to enter and turn around in. Then she left the den and walked several yards to where a spring bubbled fresh, cool water from the earth. The wolf stood in the narrow stream that flowed from the spring, letting the cold wetness wash over her feet. After lapping up long drinks of the water, she returned to the den and crawled in, turned in a tight circle, then lay down with a sigh. It would be many hours before she would come out again.

PHOTO: HILARY COOLEY, US FISH AND WILDLIFE SERVICE.

Wolf pups emerging from den.

The labor began that afternoon and continued into the night. The black wolf had never birthed puppies before, but she went about the work as if she were an experienced mother. The contractions came hard, causing her body to bear down as each pup entered the birth canal. Once each pup emerged, the black wolf licked it clean of the thin membrane surrounding it. Her vigorous licking not only cleaned the pups but stimulated their breathing as well. She shredded the umbilical cord with her teeth carefully, so it would not bleed too much. The umbilical cord had carried nutrition from the placenta to the baby, but her milk would feed them now. The pups came in intervals of around one to three hours, allowing her body time to rest in between. Each birth was followed by the delivery of the placenta, which the mother wolf consumed. This provided protein for her hard-working body and kept away predators that might smell the afterbirth and come searching for food. By morning, the den was filled with whining pups, all intent on nursing. The labor of delivery was done, but the work of the wolf parents had just started.

The sun rose over the tops of the ponderosa pines on the hills surrounding the den site, melting the late-season frost that sparkled on the spring flowers. Journey paced around the entrance to the den, his broad feet making a well-worn path on the soft soil. During the night, he'd stuck his head into the tunnel a few times and once even crawled halfway in. But the female wolf had snarled at him as if she didn't know who he was, so he backed out and resumed his pacing. The night had been a long one for Journey as well as for the black wolf.

When the sun was high in the sky, she emerged from the den. Journey rose from his resting spot on a soft blanket of pine needles and loped

PHOTO: JOHN STEPHENSON, JUNE 2, 2014.

John Stephenson was quite close when he snapped this picture, the first photo of Journey and the black wolf's pups. Taken on June 2, 2014, the pups were around six weeks old.

over to greet her. The black wolf ignored him and went to the spring, where she took in mouthfuls of the cool water, over and over again, until her thirst was quenched. Then she hurried back to the den and crawled in without so much as touching noses with her mate. Journey watched her disappear underground. He peeked into the dark tunnel, seeing nothing, but hearing the high-pitched whines of the pups as their mother settled in.

THE PROTECTION OF WOLVES

Shortly after Journey left his homeland in the fall of 2011, his father, OR-4, and a young male wolf from the Imnaha pack were implicated in several livestock deaths. State officials decided these two wolves needed to die to prevent more cattle and sheep losses. However, three conservation groups, Cascadia Wildlands, Center for Biological Diversity, and Oregon Wild, legally challenged the state to stop the kill order on the two wolves. They believed that the elimination of these animals was in violation of the state's Endangered Species Act. They also felt that wolves had not recovered sufficiently in Oregon to allow for lethal removal, especially of a breeding male. A judge listened to the organizations and agreed with them. In the nick of time, just after a shooter missed his mark on one of the wolves, the kill order was stopped. OR-4 and the other wolf were allowed to live. Over the next several years, the Imnaha pack killed less livestock, perhaps because ranchers were learning better ways to prevent this from happening.

The Federal Endangered Species Act, which was passed into law in 1973, served to protect the gray wolf throughout the United States beginning in 1974. But as populations increased in the Rocky Mountains, officials decided that wolves could survive without these protections. Conservation groups fought against this order and lawsuits stopped the action for a time. However, in 2011 the federal government turned control of wolves over to the states that had a healthy wolf population, or a potential for it. This applied first to Idaho and Montana, then Utah, Washington, and Eastern Oregon. Eventually, Wyoming, Wisconsin, Michigan, and Minnesota followed suit.

The gray wolf was one of only two species removed from the Endangered Species List by an act of Congress rather than through a process of scientific review. The result of this decision was that the recreational hunting and trapping of wolves was made legal in several states. By the spring of 2014, when Journey's first litter of pups was born, approximately 2,800 wolves had been killed for sport in Idaho, Montana, Wyoming, Wisconsin, Michigan, and Minnesota.

FIRE

Journey and his mate paced while the pups played, chewing on sticks and each other, oblivious to the problem at hand. It had been weeks since it had rained hard, and when it had rained, the brief showers were accompanied by loud thunder and bright flashes of lightning. The most recent storm had hit four days before, and it had been a bad one, with strong winds, frequent flashes of lightning, and only a sprinkling of precipitation. One lightning strike started a forest fire, affecting all of the living creatures in the area of the Rogue River-Siskiyou National Forest, where the wolf family lived.

Dust puffed up from the hard-packed soil beneath the broad feet of the adult wolves. Grasshoppers jumped in the dry brush, the inch-long insects making a creaky vibration that sounded like unhappy rattlesnakes. Nearby, the stream that had once flowed so fully was barely a trickle as the thirsty ground soaked up the much-needed moisture. The late July air was thick with smoke, making it difficult for the wolves to see through the surrounding cedars and pines. The smoke stung the sensitive membranes inside their nostrils as Journey and his mate sniffed, trying to determine if it was time to move the pups.

The pair had traveled with their young to this spot in early June. The pups had outgrown their den, and this area provided a safe place for them to explore and play while their parents hunted. The new home, known as a rendezvous site, was in an open valley surrounded by tall trees on three sides. Several large, flat boulders on a hill at the edge of the site provided Journey with a place to survey his surroundings.

Traveling from the den to the rendezvous site had taken a long time, even though it was only a mile. Journey led the way, meandering through the wilderness in search of a likely spot, while the mother wolf lagged behind to keep track of the pups. Many interesting things were discovered on this first trip into the outer world. A butterfly distracted one pup, which chased the monarch until she was so far away from her family that she couldn't be seen. Mother wolf took off after her daughter and led the way back to the pack.

Another pup noticed a unique smell on the ground below a tree and he took to digging. The other wolves didn't notice his absence until the pup, frightened by being alone, sat down and howled, bringing the others in a dead run to find him. When the pack finally stopped at the new home site, the adult wolves had to be strict parents, using growls and snarls to keep the pups from straying. By nightfall, the youngsters were too worn out to wander, and they nestled close together to sleep, just like they had in the narrow confines of the den.

Shortly after their arrival at the rendezvous site, the afternoon sun hung high in the sky, tinged red by the heavy smoke from the forest fire that raged nearby. Journey walked to the edge of the meadow, gazing into the forest. The wind picked up, moving the long guard hairs on the top of his neck and back. As it did, the dense air cleared a little. The wind gusted again, lifting the dark cloud of smoke from the sky. It fueled the fire a few miles away, shifting the flames in the opposite direction, where they burned acres and acres of dry forest and the buildings that stood in their path. The fire was moving away. The wolves could stay where they were. Journey returned to the meadow to lie on the cool surface of a smooth boulder. He took a deep breath and settled in for a long nap.*

US Fish and Wildlife Service trail camera photo of one of the three known pups born to Journey and his mate was taken on July 12, 2014.

PHOTO: US FISH AND WILDLIFE SERVICE TRAIL CAMERA, JULY 12, 2014.

NATURE KNOWS BEST

This wasn't the first fire Journey had experienced. While he spent time in California, a large one had burned thousands of acres near him, yet

* The Oregon Gulch fire burned over 36,000 acres in July of 2014 in Southern Oregon and Northern California. The area affected was only a few miles from where Journey's pack was known to be at the time.

PHOTO: SGT. KEONAONA PAULO, US MARINE CORPS.

A California hillside ablaze.

he remained close to the edge of the fire. While it is difficult to know exactly how a wild animal reacts to forest fires, we know that few of them die because of them. With senses much more acute than ours, wildlife can smell, hear, and see the fire long before it reaches their location. These animals know their environment well, making escape feasible for most. Some species stay, such as reptiles and amphibians that burrow into the ground until the flames pass.

Forest fires are essential for the environment. They increase biodiversity and stimulate new plant growth. Some plant species require fires to reproduce, like the Jack pine, whose cones remain closed for years until the tree is burned and the heat from the fire opens the cones so its seeds can spread. Fires destroy dense areas, creating meadows filled with new vegetation for many species to eat. Predators such as wolves may have a feast after a fire, preying on animals as they escape the burning areas.

Nature has ways of caring for itself and its creatures. Fires help the forests and grasslands stay healthy. Predators and the animals they eat exist together in ways that keep them both strong and fit. People have much to learn from nature and its creatures, including *Canis lupus*, a species that has existed for millions of years in a wide variety of environments. Wolves are survivors, if we will only allow them to be.

END OF AN ERA

The battery on Journey's GPS collar finally wore out sometime in 2015, although the VHF component continued to function. This meant a person searching for OR-7 needed to be near him to get a signal from the wolf's collar. Journey's GPS had lasted for six years, much longer than was expected. His family was officially known as the Rogue pack now, named after the upper Rogue River watershed where they lived. The biologists overseeing these wolves hoped to recapture OR-7 and replace his collar. If they couldn't catch Journey, they would capture his mate and collar her. If one of the pups was caught, it would be collared as well. Young wolves could be safely collared as long as they were large enough that they did not outgrow their collars. The plan was to use a safe foothold trap to secure the animal. Then a long pole with a tranquilizer dart at the end would be used to sedate the wolf. Once sedated, the wolf would be thoroughly checked out and a new collar applied.

The biologists spent hours in the field, carefully setting traps and waiting for wolves to step into them. But despite all their efforts, it didn't happen. The Rogue pack just didn't want to be caught.

Some people feel that wolves should be left alone, without collars that track their every move. While great care is used when sedating wolves, there is always a chance the medication can be harmful. Journey's sister, who was tranquilized on the same day he was, was found dead shortly afterward, perhaps from effects of the capture. On the other hand, radio collars are a window into the lives of wolves. If OR-7 had not been collared, we would know very little about his long and challenging trip from northeastern Oregon to California and then back into Oregon. The information we have gained has taught us all a lot about wolves and their ways. And Journey's fascinating story has enlisted support

PHOTO: ODFW TRAIL CAMERA, DECEMBER 4, 2014.

This ODFW trail camera picture of an uncollared Snake River pack member was taken on December 4, 2014.

*   *What do you think? Should wolves be collared so we can study them, or should they be left alone and away from the scrutiny of human beings?*

for wolves from people around the globe who want these animals to remain a part of our environment.*

The radio signal on Journey's mother, OR-2, or Sophie, stopped emitting signals in the summer of 2013. She was not with the Imnaha wolves when Roblyn and Russ surveyed the pack. It was assumed that Sophie had died. She was nine years old, a long life span for a wild wolf. And what a life she lived! Sophie crossed the Snake River in 2008 and met up with OR-4, or perhaps entered Oregon with him. In the years they were together, Sophie and OR-4 produced at least four litters of pups and several of these wolves, like OR-7, dispersed to distant locations in Oregon and California. Sophie and OR-4 are nearly as famous as Journey for all they have done to return wolves to the landscape of the Pacific Northwest.

After Sophie was gone, OR-4 paired up with gray female OR-39, also known as Limpy. She earned this name because of an injured leg that caused her to walk with a limp. The pair had a litter together in 2014 and all seemed fine. However, OR-4 was nearly ten years old, and aging wolves have a difficult time surviving in the wild. Their teeth become dull or fall out. They are not as fast as they once were. And there is competition from other members of the pack to take over the role of breeding animals. This may be why OR-4 and Limpy, along with their two yearling pups, wandered into a rancher's calving grounds to find food. In a three-week period in March of 2016, four calves and one sheep were killed and consumed. Investigations by the Oregon Department of Fish and Wildlife found that OR-4 and OR-39 were responsible for all of these livestock deaths.

On the morning of March 31, 2016, a helicopter rose into the blue skies of Wallowa County to search

PHOTO: ODFW.

OR-4, as captured by remote camera. May 18, 2013.

for wolves. But this time it was not to catch and collar them or to do the annual survey to determine how many wolves were living in the state. This time the goal was to find OR-4, OR-39, and their two offspring and shoot them. The Imnaha breeding pair had crossed a fatal line. According to the Oregon Wolf Conservation and Management Plan, wolves could be killed for proven livestock depredation under certain conditions, and all of these conditions had been met. There was no escape for the wolves this time. Wildlife managers are expected to not only look out for wolves and other animals, but also to protect the interest of people, including livestock producers. Russ Morgan said in a press release that, "This is the tough part of the job, but we believe lethal control is the right decision in this case."

Many people grieved over the loss of these wolves, the core of the Imnaha pack. But the legacy of OR-4 and OR-2 is carried on by their offspring as these wolves continue to disperse throughout Oregon and into California.

TIME ALONE

Journey trotted southeast at a steady pace. The sun had fallen, leaving the forest a place of shadows and dark shapes. But the wolf's vision was sharp, allowing him to weave around the tree trunks and over the fallen logs and volcanic rocks that littered the forest floor. He was nearly seven years old. While he was still a fast and accomplished hunter, there were times when his offspring brought prey down while he watched from the sidelines.

By midnight, Journey reached his destination on the bank of the Klamath River, a salmon-filled ribbon of water that begins at Upper Klamath Lake and travels 260 miles to the Pacific Ocean, picking up

PHOTO: TUPPER ANSEL BLAKE, US FISH AND WILDLIFE SERVICE.

The Klamath River, winding through a valley.

streams and feeding lakes as it flows. He soaked his paws in the mud at the edge of the river, alert to the sound and smell of humans camping a good distance to the south. He smelled a potential food source and moved up the bank to investigate. Digging through a thin layer of fallen leaves, he uncovered the remains of a rainbow trout that had been tossed aside by a fisherman. Journey picked a few mouthfuls and then took in several bites of long, green grass to settle his stomach.

The crunch of vehicle tires on the gravel of the nearby road grew louder and then was quiet, followed by voices from the camping humans. Journey left the riverbank and climbed a steep ridge. This was a place he knew well. Many times, before the black wolf and the pups, he had rested on this ridge, observing the course of the Klamath, and the humans that fished the river and camped near its shores, as well the deer that quenched their thirst with the clean, cool water. Journey studied the scene below for a long while and then turned in a tight circle, lay down, and tucked his nose beneath his tail to sleep.

The next morning, before the March sun had fully risen, Journey killed a young buck that was browsing on willow branches in a meadow near the river. The hunt had been an easy one. The wolf surprised the deer and had it on the ground before the animal had time to react and run. He fed first on the internal organs, then the muscle and flesh. Within three days, the carcass was nothing but scattered bones, hooves, hide, and tufts of hair.

Journey returned to the ridge after feeding on the deer for the final time. The campers and fishers were gone, and the Klamath River was quiet except for the honking of Canada geese as a small flock of the birds returned to these lands. Journey settled in on a soft spot of the earth and dozed until awakened by the light of the full moon. He stood and shook the dust from his coat. Then he moved into a trot, then a lope, his way illuminated by the bright moonlight. He made the trip in half the time it took him to get to the river, running as though he were hungry, which he wasn't, or as if others were waiting for his return, which they were.

His family had grown over the last two years. Last spring, his black mate had birthed another litter of pups, and now she was heavy with her third litter. Their offspring were as large as Journey and his mate, and the ones that had not dispersed did their part to help care for their siblings and bring down game for the family to eat. The pack had settled in a remote area of the Rogue River-Siskiyou National Forest. Few humans saw them. Journey had not forgotten the fear he felt when in the presence of people. He kept his family far away from them.

The black wolf heard him before she caught his scent. His movement in the forest awakened the pups, and they rose, stretched, and gathered for the attack. They sprang on Journey the second he entered the clearing, nearly knocking him down. He joined in the welcoming ceremony, licking the noses of his mate and pups, rubbing his head with theirs, his tail wagging like a flag in a furious wind. The family became a mass of wolves, moving together across the plateau of the den site as if stuck together with glue. Their voices broke out in whines and whimpers. One yearling pup let loose a howl.

Worn out from the excitement, the family drifted off to find comfortable spots to finish their night's sleep. Journey and the black wolf settled in a few feet from each other, tails touching as they settled in on the pine needle–covered ground. The wolves slept well that night. Journey was home.

PHOTO: US FISH AND WILDLIFE SERVICE TRAIL CAMERA, FEBRUARY 26, 2016.

This photo was taken on February 26, 2016, by a US Fish and Wildlife Service trail camera. Journey is the one with the collar. The wolf behind him is one of his pups, as large as Journey and looking just like him.

The Journey Continues

The wolves kept coming. In August of 2015, trail cameras set out by the California Department of Fish and Wildlife captured images of two adult wolves and five pups in the northern part of the state, beneath the shadows of 14,000-foot high Mount Shasta. This was the first pack of wild wolves known to exist in California in nearly one hundred years. The black-coated family group was named the Shasta pack and biologists set out to gather scat samples to determine where the wolves had come from. When the samples were analyzed, we learned that the breeding pair were both from the Imnaha pack in northeastern Oregon, making them siblings to Journey.

OR-25, a lanky, black male wearing a GPS collar, also left the Imnaha pack of northeastern Oregon and headed south. He spent time on the Warm Springs Indian Reservation and then was traced to Southern Oregon. He took a stroll into Northern California, but soon turned around and headed back to Oregon, staying in the same general vicinity as the Rogue pack. In autumn of 2015, OR-3, a large black wolf long lost to biologists, was seen north of Crater Lake. OR-3 is Journey's older brother, from the first known litter of OR-4 and OR-2. On June 22, 2016, a trail camera captured images of OR-3, looking long and lean in his summer coat, being followed by a gray pup. At eight years of age, OR-3 had paired with another dispersing northeastern Oregon wolf, OR-28, and

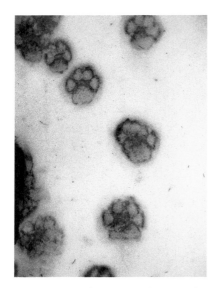

Joe Kreuzman is an experienced wild animal tracker and director of the Coyote Trails School of Nature in Medford, Oregon. Joe and his dog, Taru, were out hiking the day after Thanksgiving in 2014 when they came across these fresh tracks that could be made by no other than Journey's Rogue pack. Needless to say, Joe was thrilled. In his words, "To a tracker, there is no better day."

produced a litter of pups. They were called the Silver Lake wolves. The Oregon Department of Fish and Wildlife does not use a pack name until there are at least four wolves traveling together during winter. OR-33, another black Imnaha wolf, also made his way down Journey's well-worn path. OR-33 earned the dubious distinction of being the first wolf to prey on livestock in Southern Oregon in over seventy years. Fladry was quickly strung around the livestock pens to scare OR-33 away.

Along with the Imnaha wolves, members of other northeastern Oregon packs have also made the same long journey, their presence discovered through trail cameras and rare sightings. Why did these wolves all venture down the long and dangerous path that led them to southwestern Oregon and Northern California? Some believe a scent trail was laid by Journey that was followed, even years later, by other wolves. Wolves have a sense of smell over a hundred times stronger than a human's. And they leave their scent without even trying to, through glands on the pads of their paws, as well as in their urine and feces. And according to Roblyn Brown, serving as Oregon's Acting Wolf Coordinator, "Wolves tend to use the landscape in similar ways. We have seen wolves following the same topography and crossing barriers and obstacles at the same place."

Imagine yourself on a very long, difficult scavenger hunt, with clues scattered here and there, some very far apart. You don't give up and you manage to stay on the path by finding clues that keep you moving in the right direction. The prize at the end of the scavenger hunt is an oasis, a beautiful land that your neighbors and family members have already discovered, and in this land you find safe shelter and plenty of good food for everyone to eat. Your challenging journey, like the journey of the wolves that traveled to Southern Oregon and Northern California, proves to be worth all of the effort it took to get there.

OR-7 has been a trailblazer in the return of wolves to their historic homelands in Oregon and California. It is likely that wolves will continue to follow his lead, as well as the paths of other wolves, and expand their range even farther into other states. The future will reveal if humans allow for this expansion and find ways to live with wolves. Will we seek solutions to the livestock issues that go hand in hand with wild predators? Will we work to protect the large areas of wilderness that wolves need to exist in? Will human hunters allow four-legged predators their fair share of game, understanding that wolves do not destroy ungulate populations? And will we come to appreciate that the very presence of wolves helps to return the wild to a more natural and healthy state? These are questions for all of us to ponder in the years to come. Hopefully, it won't be long before the answers are all a resounding "Yes!"

PHOTO: CALIFORNIA DEPARTMENT OF FISH AND WILDLIFE TRAIL CAMERA, AUGUST 2015.

This August 2015 picture of the Shasta pack was taken by a trail camera set by the California Department of Fish and Wildlife.

WHAT YOU CAN DO TO HELP JOURNEY AND OTHER WOLVES

There is no single way to ensure protection for wolves. Our world is a complicated place, one that must meet the needs of humans as well as animals. But there is room for both if we are willing to compromise and live a lifestyle that lessens our impact on the earth and its creatures.

One way we can all help prevent the destruction of wolves is by educating ourselves and others about them. *Canis lupus* has been burdened with bad publicity for thousands of years. Even some modern movies show the wolf as a vicious and dangerous animal, something

we know not to be true. As we talk with others about the importance of wolves in the natural world, of their complex social structure and deep intelligence and how they do little harm to humans and other species, the word will spread and people will become more aware of the truth.

Passing laws to protect wolves and other wildlife is very effective. You can write or call state legislators, Congress members, governors, and other decision makers to make sure your voice is heard. Gathering signatures on petitions and organizing public events to gain publicity are also helpful methods of educating the public, as well as politicians and public servants.

We have a powerful means of influencing decisions that affect wolves and other animals by making careful decisions about the products we purchase. We can refuse to buy items made of fur. By doing so, we reduce the number of wild creatures that suffer from trapping, as well as those raised in captivity for their fur. If we eat meat, we can choose to buy it from producers who try to prevent problems between predators and livestock rather than killing the offending animal. This is called wildlife-friendly ranching. Some producers are using a label to tell consumers that they support the protection of wolves, coyotes, and other species.

PHOTO: US FISH AND WILDLIFE SERVICE TRAIL CAMERA, JULY 12, 2016.

This pair of young wolves are from the 2016 Rogue pack litter.

Money is essential to saving wildlife. Even small donations to organizations such as Oregon Wild, Defenders of Wildlife, Center for Biological Diversity, and Cascadia Wildlands are beneficial. The money we give to these nonprofit groups goes to educating the public, paying for legal protections for wolves, and supporting staff people who devote their lives to saving wolves. Spending money at wolf sanctuaries, zoos, and other places where wolves live, including Yellowstone National Park, is helpful as well. When tourism dollars come from people who want to watch wolves and not shoot them, officials see the value in preserving these unique and important animals.

PHOTO: MEL CLEMENTS.

Mel Clements wasn't looking for wolves when he snapped this picture early in the morning on July 13, 2016, on the Dead Indian Plateau east of Ashland, Oregon. Mel, a photographer who specializes in birds, was searching for the rare great gray owl, the largest species of owl by length in the Northern Hemisphere. But this young black wolf suddenly appeared in a meadow often inhabited by great gray owls. Mel shared the photo with authorities and was told his subject may be one of the Keno wolves that are known to live in this area.

If you're still deciding what you want to do with your life, consider a career that will help you help wolves. You could become a biologist, an attorney, a leader of a nonprofit organization, a teacher, a park ranger, or perhaps a writer who spreads the word about the value of wolves. But know that in any job you do, there are many ways to help make this a better world for animals, for the environment, and for other people.

THE LAW FOR THE WOLVES

by Rudyard Kipling
(1865–1936)

Now this is the law of the jungle, as old and as true as the sky,
And the wolf that shall keep it may prosper, but the wolf that shall break it must die.

As the creeper that girdles the tree trunk, the law runneth forward and back;
For the strength of the pack is the wolf, and the strength of the wolf is the pack.

Wash daily from nose tip to tail tip; drink deeply, but never too deep;
And remember the night is for hunting and forget not the day is for sleep.

The jackal may follow the tiger, but, cub, when thy whiskers are grown,
Remember the wolf is a hunter—go forth and get food of thy own.

Keep peace with the lords of the jungle, the tiger, the panther, the bear;
And trouble not Hathi the Silent, and mock not the boar in his lair.

When pack meets with pack in the jungle, and neither will go from the trail,
Lie down till the leaders have spoken; it may be fair words shall prevail.

When ye fight with a wolf of the pack ye must fight him alone and afar,
Lest others take part in the quarrel and the pack is diminished by war.

The lair of the wolf is his refuge, and where he has made him his home,
Not even the head wolf may enter, not even the council may come.

The lair of the wolf is his refuge, but where he has digged it too plain,
The council shall send him a message, and so he shall change it again.

If ye kill before midnight be silent and wake not the woods with your bay,
Lest ye frighten the deer from the crop and thy brothers go empty away.

Ye may kill for yourselves, and your mates, and your cubs as they need and ye can;
But kill not for pleasure of killing, and seven times never kill man.

If ye plunder his kill from a weaker, devour not all in thy pride,
Pack-right is the right of the meanest; so leave him the head and the hide.

The kill of the pack is the meat of the pack. Ye must eat where it lies;
And no one may carry away of that meat to his lair, or he dies.

The kill of the wolf is the meat of the wolf. He may do what he will,
But, till he is given permission, the pack may not eat of that kill.

Lair right is the right of the mother. From all of her years she may claim
One haunch of each kill for her litter, and none may deny her the same.

Cub right is the right of the yearling. From all of his pack he may claim
Full gorge when the killer has eaten; and none may refuse him the same.

Cave right is the right of the father, to hunt by himself for his own;
He is freed from all calls to the pack. He is judged by the council alone.

Because of his age and his cunning, because of his gripe and his paw,
In all that the law leaveth open the word of the head wolf is law.

Now these are the laws of the jungle, and many and mighty are they;
But the head and the hoof of the law and the haunch and the hump is—Obey!

SOURCE NOTES

BY PAGE NUMBER

CHAPTER ONE: THE BEGINNING

1–2   Details of the size, eye color, and behavior of wolf pups came from *The Wolf Almanac* by Robert H. Busch, p. 82.

3   Journey's celebrity status and other events of his life can be found in detail on the website of Oregon Wild: http://www.oregonwild.org.

3   Details on number of air miles traveled by OR-7 came from communication with staff of the California Department of Fish and Wildlife. The more than 4,000 miles Journey traveled included 3,300 miles in California, and he accumulated much of this distance traveling from one scent post to another, checking for evidence of other wolves.

4–5   The acclaimed book *Of Wolves and Men* by Barry Lopez provided historical information on wolves in the US See pp. 169–198.

6   The topic of trophic cascades and wolves is being studied by several scientists, including William J. Ripple and R. L. Beschta of Oregon State University. They and others have written about this topic in many publications. Here is a link to one article that was published in the journal *Ecology*. Your librarian can help you search for it: Painter, L. E, R. L. Beschta, E. J. Larsen, and W. J. Ripple. 2015. "Recovering aspen follow changing elk dynamics in Yellowstone: evidence of a trophic cascade?" *Ecology* 96(1): 252–263.

6   Mary Ellen Hannibal's wonderful book *The Spine of the Continent* teaches about keystone species on pages 109, 120, and elsewhere.

7   Quotes from Amaroq Weiss are used with her permission and come from various media sources. Learn more about Amaroq and her work on the website of the Center for Biological Diversity at http://www.biologicaldiversity.org/.

7   Much has been published on the return of wolves to Yellowstone National Park and Central Idaho. See the Further Reading list for books to read about this fascinating time.

8   This Forest Service website has information on the history of the Nez Perce in the Hells Canyon area: http://www.fs.usda.gov/main/npnht/home.

8–9   The information on OR-2 (Sophie) can be found on the website of the Oregon Department of Fish and Wildlife (ODFW) at http://www.dfw.state.or.us/wolves/.

CHAPTER TWO: GROWING UP

11–12   Wolves love to play, whether they are young or old. I observed this with the wolves under my care, and I read about their play in the book *Among Wolves* by Gordon Haber and Marybeth Holleman, pp. 86–88. The details on pup size and regurgitation can be found in *The Wolf Almanac*, pp. 84–85.

13–14   Much of this information came from a personal interview with Roblyn Brown at the ODFW office in La Grande, Oregon, in October 2012.

14   I must thank my friends Pam and Randy Comeleo for teaching me about GPS. The Comeleos are advocates for coyotes and other animals in northwestern Oregon.

15   Statistics on the successful taking of prey come from *Decade of the Wolf*, *The Wolf Almanac*, and other sources.

15–17   I did some online research to learn more about the habits of elk, as well as the meaning of the word *wapiti*. And, again, Gordon Haber's work, as documented in *Among Wolves*, provided in-depth material about how young wolves learn to hunt. They are not born knowing how to bring down an elk, and it takes a lot of time and patience from the adults for pups to become accomplished at this difficult skill. Please see pp. 73–76 in *Among Wolves* for more information.

17–18   I learned these details during my interview with Roblyn Brown.

19–20   We don't know how a wolf feels after being darted with a tranquilizer gun, but we can assume it creates a fear response. And I imagine it would do anything to shed the cumbersome collar from around its neck! Details on the sense of smell of wolves came from *The Wolf Almanac*, pp. 32–24.

20   You can read about the famous Druid Peak pack in *Decade of the Wolf: Returning the Wild to Yellowstone* by Douglas W. Smith and Gary Ferguson. The Druids were once the largest pack of wolves known, as noted on page 81.

20–21   Information on pack structure and dispersal can be found in many sources, including *Neither God Nor Devil: Rethinking Our Perception of Wolves* by Eva-Lena Rehnmark.

CHAPTER THREE: THE JOURNEY BEGINS

24   The date of Journey's dispersal can be found on the website of the Oregon Department of Fish and Wildlife (ODFW) http://www.dfw.state.or.us/wolves/.

25   *The Spine of the Continent* by Mary Ellen Hannibal tells the story of the pronghorn antelope migration beginning on page 202. This book also discusses the effort to create a protected path for animals that runs the entire length of North America.

26–27   Oregon Wild's website has lots of great information about Journey, including how he was named in the contest they sponsored: http://www.oregonwild.org.

27–28   We know that Journey traveled through Crater Lake National Park, as his tracks were seen and GPS readings placed him there. We don't know for sure if he ventured to the edge of the lake as in my story, but if you were a wolf, wouldn't you? I watched the wolves in my care play with ice during the cold Iowa winters. Also, *The Hidden Life of Wolves* by Jim and Jamie Dutcher shares how wolves play with ice on page 100 and elsewhere.

29   News about Journey feasting on an elk carcass came from a newspaper article by Mark Freeman in the Medford Mail Tribune on December 18, 2011. http://www.mailtribune.com/article/20111218/NEWS/112180317.

29–30   I learned about Liz Parrish's encounter with OR-7 through my interview with her, newspaper articles, and on the Crystalwood Lodge website.

31   While having lunch at a café near Little Hyatt Lake, I was told by a waiter that a customer had reported seeing the wandering wolf. The waiter said he had also spotted a wolf while hiking the PCT, and this was years before Journey made his way to Southern Oregon. There have been several wolf sightings in the area, making me wonder if wolves have been around longer than we thought.

33–34   Learn more about coyotes on the Project Coyote website: http://www.projectcoyote.org/about/. You can read about coyote and wolf interactions in *The Wolf Almanac*, pp. 64–65.

34–35   Information on how the second photo of Journey came about was from a newspaper article (http://www.sfgate.com/science/article/California-s-lone-wolf-seen-mingling-with-coyotes-3554309.php), as well as through correspondence with the California Department of Fish and Wildlife.

35–37   *The Hidden Life of Wolves* gives a thorough review of non-lethal measures on pp. 163–170.

CHAPTER FOUR: SETTLING IN

39–40   The story of Mark and Jennifer Vargas came from an article in the newspaper (http://www.mailtribune.com/article/20130405/LIFE/304050306), and details were verified with Mark through emails.

41   When wolves meet, it is not likely to be love at first sight! Journey and the black female would have been on their guard and perhaps territorial. I made the assumption that Journey took on the dominant role and displayed this by his raised hackles, stiff gait, and high tail carriage. The female may well have run, and when caught, she may have acted submissive by rolling over and licking Journey on the muzzle. But once the roles were figured out, the two wolves got along, obviously.

42   News that Journey had found a mate traveled quickly. One article appeared in *National Geographic* on March, 18, 2014. http://news.nationalgeographic.com/news/2014/05/140516-wolves-oregon-or7-science-endangered-species-animals/.

43   The information on scatology, the study of scat, came from my own experience doing this (yes, I used a stick!), as well as some online research. ODFW's website shared the news on results of DNA studies on Journey's mate. I read a great article on dogs being trained to find scat in the Jan/Feb 2016 issue of *Sierra* magazine. It was written by Julian Smith and called "Sit, Stay, Track."

44–45   I know from personal experience that female wolves don't like their partners around when giving birth. This is a time when they must focus on the job at hand. Details of the birth process came from my younger sister, Michelle Elgin-Kolbeck. She has helped human babies come into the world as well as a litter of poodles.

46–47   Information on losses of wolves to hunting and the EPA came from my own knowledge and more online research. These details are a challenge to keep up with, as laws affecting the protection of wolves change frequently and vary from state to state.

47–49   How animals react to forest fire is a curiosity to me. We know some about this, but it is not possible to fully understand what an animal senses and understands when the world around them is going up in flames. I did learn a lot about how wild animals escape harm as well as the benefit of forest fires from Oregon Wild Northeast Oregon field coordinator Rob Klavins. He helped set my concerns about Journey's safety at ease.

50–51   Information about the recollaring efforts came from listening to John Stephenson, US Fish and Wildlife Service, during the 2015 Oregon Wild Wolf Rendezvous at Crater Lake.

52   I learned about the livestock losses and the lethal removal of OR-4 and his family from the ODFW website, as well as from talking with wolf advocate Wally Sykes. This was a difficult time for everyone who cared about wolves, including the biologists involved.

53   It seemed likely that Journey would need a little time to himself. Wolves often wander on their own and come back to their pack when ready to. And what better place to go than the lovely Klamath River, a place where my son fly-fishes and where we've seen peregrine falcons swooping into their cliff-side nests to feed their young. The Klamath is a short jaunt for an active wolf like Journey and a river he crossed before entering California. I only hope his mate took some day trips too!

EPILOGUE

57   Information on the dispersing wolves can be found on the websites of both the Oregon and California Departments of Fish and Wildlife. Also, a new website called Pacific Wolf Family (https://pacificwolffamily.org) is a one-stop shop to learn about wolves in Oregon, California, and Washington.

58   This quote from Roblyn Brown was found on the Facebook page of ODFW Conservation on July 28, 2016.

GLOSSARY

Advocate	A person who supports a certain cause. An example is someone who stands up for the welfare of wolves.
Bounty	A reward given by a governing agency for some specific act, such as killing a wild animal.
Biodiversity	The vast variety of life on earth, including plants, animals, and the environment they exist in.
Biologist	One who has trained to study living organisms, including plants and animals.
Browse	The term for the feeding on woody plants, like trees and shrubs. For example, deer and other ungulates browse on willow trees, eating the leaves, bark, and branches.
Caldera	A volcanic crater formed by an eruption that led to the collapse of the mouth of the volcano.
Canis lupus	The scientific name for wolves. Using a system called binomial nomenclature, organisms are known by two names. The gray wolf is: *Canis* (the genus) *lupus* (the species). This system was first created in the mid-1700s by Carolus Linnaeus, a Swedish botanist. Using Latin terms, he developed a framework of seven parts to identify all plants and animals. The seven parts are: kingdom, phylum, class, order, family, genus, and species. The system is still used today, with some variations.

Carrion	The decaying flesh of dead animals. Carrion is an important food source for many animals, including wolves.
Coexist	When populations of difference species exist in the same habitat. They may not always get along, and one may be the predator and the other the prey, but they inhabit the same environment over a period of time.
Depredation	In this text, the term depredation means "to prey upon." The word is used to refer to predators preying upon livestock.
DNA studies	Deoxyribonucleic acid, or DNA, lives in the nucleus of cells. DNA carries the genetic information that makes us who we are. Scientific studies of the DNA from wild animals teaches about the individual animals, their populations, and their behavior. DNA can be taken from blood, hair, scat, and other methods. Samples reveal the genetic makeup of the animal it came from, as with the Shasta pack in California. We now know that these wolves came from the same pack as OR-7.
Disperse	To move in different directions, to scatter. Young wolves routinely disperse to other locations, sometimes far away from home.

Endangered Species Act	Signed into law in 1973, the ESA protects rare and endangered species. Although not a perfect solution, the ESA has helped to increase the numbers of many animals and plants, including bison, peregrine falcons, black-footed ferrets, and the San Clemente Island Indian paintbrush.
Extinction	The death of an entire species. While gray wolves have been extirpated (gone from a certain area) in much of their territory, some species, such as the Tasmanian wolf, are gone forever.
Fladry	Flag-like strips placed around livestock enclosures to frighten predators away. If electricity is added, the term turbo-fladry is used.
Guard hair	The long, shiny outer hairs on a wolf's coat that shed rain and snow and help protect the wolf. Along with the undercoat, the guard hairs grow long in the winter and shed out in the spring. Wolves look much larger in the winter months when wearing their full coats.
Gene pool	The genetic makeup of a specific population. In order for a species to continue, there must be sufficient diversity in the gene pool. Captive breeding programs for red and Mexican wolves are carefully breeding animals to make sure they are not all from the same parents in order to keep the gene pool diverse.

GPS	Global Positioning System. Receives signals transmitted by satellites orbiting earth. The GPS unit stores information that is uploaded through a satellite and sent to a computer. There, the readings show up as dots on a map on the computer screen.
Habitat	The place where a species (plant, animal, or other type of organism) normally lives. The habitat is where the living being can find food, shelter, a mate, and protection.
Iditarod	A grueling 1,000-mile long dog sled race that runs from Anchorage, in Southcentral Alaska, to Nome, which is on the Bering Sea coast. The Iditarod is held annually in early March. The 2016 winner, Dallas Seavey, set a record for completing the race in 8 days, 11 hours, 20 minutes, and 16 seconds.
Keystone species	A species, such as wolves and beavers, that is uniquely essential to its habitat. If it is removed, major changes occur in the environment.
Livestock guardian dogs	Large breeds of dogs that are used to protect livestock (usually sheep and cattle) from predators.
Milk teeth	The teeth wolves have when young. The milk teeth fall out and are completely replaced by permanent adult teeth (42 of them compared to 32 in humans) by the time the pups are about six or seven months old.

Nonprofit organization	An organization that is set up to benefit a certain cause, such as the protection of wildlife. Unlike a for-profit organization, the goal of nonprofits is to work for their cause rather than make a profit.
Pacific Crest Trail	Officially completed in 1993, the PCT is a hiking and equestrian trail that extends 2,650 miles from Mexico to Canada.
Predator	An animal that preys on and consumes other animals.
Radio tracking telemetry	A way that biologists track wild animals. As with OR-7, an animal is captured and fitted with a device (GPS or VHF) that gives information on its travels. Falconers and dog handlers also use telemetry to keep track of their birds or dogs while in the field.
Raptor	Birds of prey that hunt food using their feet. Raptor comes from a Latin word that means "to seize and carry away."
Regurgitate	To vomit. Wolves regurgitate as a way of feeding young pups; not how most of us like to have our dinner served!
Rendezvous site	Derived from a French word meaning "meeting place," a rendezvous site is where adult wolves take their young to spend their first summer learning how to be big wolves. The adult wolves go on hunts while the pups stay back, often watched over by an older sibling or other family member.

Roadless area	Areas on public land where road building is limited in order to keep the land as natural as possible.
Rut	The time of year when ungulates mate. This occurs in the autumn. Male ungulates that are normally mild-mannered can become very dangerous this time of year.
Scat	The scientific term for wild animal feces.
Territory	In wolf talk, territory refers to the land that a pack feeds on and is willing to defend. The size of a wolf pack's territory varies a great deal. In Alaska, these territories have been as much as 800 square miles. In more populated places like Minnesota, they are smaller, usually less than 100 square miles.
Trail camera	Also known as camera traps, these popular devices are used to capture pictures in a remote setting. Usually, the subject is wildlife. For an aerial view, drones are fitted with cameras to photograph animals below. In Denmark, eagles are being trained to capture flying drones, in case they pose a danger to people.
Trophic cascades	The term for how predators affect their environment. The influence (or lack of one if the predator is gone) of a top predator "cascades" to other elements of their environment, including their prey.

Undercoat	The soft, fluffy, light-colored hairs that lay closest to the wolf's body. In spring, shedding wolves look quite scruffy as patches of undercoat loosen and hang on until they finally fall out or are pulled off by nature's hairbrushes: bushes, bark, twigs, and grasses.
Ungulate	An animal with hooves. The hoof may be solid or split. Ungulates are typically herbivores, or plant-eating animals.
VHF	Very high frequency signals that are picked up by an antenna.
Wapiti	A term for elk. The word is derived from the Cree and Shawnee word for "white rump."
Wildlife corridors	Connecting links of safe habitat for wildlife to travel across. These corridors allow animals to naturally migrate, to disperse to new locations, and to meet up with others of their own kind from other populations.

FURTHER READING
FOR ALL AGES

Askins, Rene. *Shadow Mountain: A Memoir of Wolves, A Woman, and the Wild*. New York: Anchor Books, 2002.

Bass, Rick. *The New Wolves: The Return of the Mexican Wolf*. Guilford: The Lyons Press, 1998.

Beeland, T. Delene. *The Secret World of Red Wolves: The Fight to Save North American's Other Wolf*. Chapel Hill: The University of North Carolina Press, 2013.

Busch, Robert H. *The Wolf Almanac*. Guilford: The Lyons Press, 2007.

Connolly, Brian A. *Alphy, A Yellowstone Wolf Pup*. College Station: Virtual Bookworm Publishing, 2013. Illustrated by George Bumann.

Crisler, Lois. *Arctic Wild: The Remarkable True Story of One Couple's Adventure Living Among Wolves*. New York: Harper and Row, 1958.

———. *Captive Wild: One Woman's Adventure Living With Wolves*. New York: Harper and Row, 1968.

Dutcher, Jim, and Jamie Dutcher. *The Hidden Life of Wolves*. Washington, DC: National Geographic Society, 2013.

———. *A Friend for Lakota: The Incredible True Story of a Wolf Who Braved Bullying*. Washington, DC: National Geographic Society, 2015.

Eisenberg, Cristina. *The Wolf's Tooth: Keystone Predators, Trophic Cascades, and Biodiversity*. Washington, DC: The Island Press, 2010.

Elgin, Robert. *The Tiger Is My Brother*. New York: William Morrow, 1980.

George, Jean Craighead. *Julie of the Wolves*. New York: Harper and Row, 1974.

———. *The Moon of the Gray Wolves*. New York: Thomas Y. Crowell Company, 1969.

Haber, Gorden, and Marybeth Holleman. *Among Wolves*. Fairbanks: University of Alaska Press, 2013.

Hall, Elizabeth. *Child of the Wolves*. New York: Houghton Mifflin, 1998.

Jans, Nick. *A Wolf Called Romeo*. New York: Houghton Mifflin, 2014.

Jazynka, Kitson, and Daniel Raven-Ellison. *Mission: Wolf Rescue: All About Wolves and How to Save Them*. Washington, DC: National Geographic Kids, 2014.

Lamplugh, Rick. *In the Temple of Wolves: A Winter's Immersion in Wild Yellowstone*. Create Space, 2014.

Lawrence, R. D. *Wolves*. San Francisco: Sierra Club Books, 1990.

London, Jonathan. *The Eyes of Gray Wolf*. San Francisco: Chronicle Books, 1993.

Lopez, Barry Holstun. *Of Wolves and Men*. New York: Charles Scriber's Sons, 1978.

McDiarmid, Gail, and Marilyn McGee. *Running for Home*. Sundog Enterprises, 2012.

Moskowitz, David. *Wolves in the Land of Salmon*. Portland: Timber Press, 2013.

Niemeyer, Carter. *Wolfer*. Boise: Bottlefly Press, 2010.

———. *Wolf Land*, Boise: Bottlefly Press, 2016.

Seidler, Tor. *Firstborn*. Atheneum Books, New York, NY, 2015.

Smith, Douglas W., and Gary Ferguson. *Decade of the Wolf: Returning the Wild to Yellowstone*. Guilford: Lyons Press, 2006.

Swinburne, Stephen. *Once a Wolf: How Wildlife Biologists Fought to Bring Back the Gray Wolf*. New York: Houghton Mifflin, 1999.

Thiel, Richard P. *Keepers of the Wolves: The Early Years of Wolf Recovery in Wisconsin*. Milwaukee: University of Wisconsin Press, 2001.

WEBSITES TO EXPLORE

California Department of Fish Wildlife: https://www.wildlife.ca.gov
/conservation/mammals/gray-wolf

Center for Biological Diversity: http://biologicaldiversity.org

Coyote Trails School of Nature: http://www.coyotetrails.org/

Defenders of Wildlife: http://www.defenders.org

International Wolf Center: http://www.wolf.org

Klamath-Siskiyou Wildlands Center: http://kswild.org

Living With Wolves: https://www.livingwithwolves.org

Oregon Department of Fish and Wildlife: http://www.dfw.state.or.us/
wolves/

Oregon Wild: http://www.oregonwild.org

Pacific Wolf Coalition: http://www.pacificwolves.org

Pacific Wolf Family: https://pacificwolffamily.org

Project Coyote: http://www.projectcoyote.org/about/

Wildlife Friendly Enterprise Network: http://wildlifefriendly.org

Wolves and Writing: https://wolvesandwriting.com

Wolves of the Rockies: http://www.wolvesoftherockies.org

Wolves in California: https://californiawolves.wordpress.com

DOCUMENTARY FILMS

Two documentary films have been made about Journey. One is called *OR7: The Journey*. This film includes footage of places OR-7 visited and interviews with people who have been important in Journey's life. A stand-in from a wolf sanctuary was used in the movie because OR-7 kept himself too hidden away to be filmed!

The other movie is called *Wolf OR-7 Expedition*, and it documents the trek of six people as they follow Journey's route from northeastern Oregon to California. These adventurers traveled 1,200 miles on foot or bicycle over mountains and through dense forests and all kinds of bad weather during their month-long expedition.

PHOTO: ASHLEY JANSSEN PHOTOGRAPHY.

This is Niwa, the wolf that played the role of Journey in the movie. Niwa lives a life of ease at the Wolf People education center in Northern Idaho.

The gray wolf known as OR-7 was born in the spring of 2009 to the Imnaha Pack. He was in a litter of at least six pups, his mother's second litter. She was spotted in 2008 after crossing the Snake River from Idaho wearing a radio tracking collar ①.

At nearly two years old, Wolf OR-7 was tagged with a GPS tracking collar by state biologists in the Wallowa Mountains. He is called OR-7 because he was Oregon's 7th collared wolf ②.

Wolf OR-7 left his pack in September 2011 to find his own territory. This is called dispersal, common for young wolves. He traveled thousands of miles, at times 30 miles a day. Wolves are shy and rarely seen by humans. We know about OR-7's dispersal only because of his GPS collar. His collar sends his location to wildlife managers via satellite signals ③. They use GPS signals to monitor wolf populations.

When OR-7 reached the Cascade Mountains, he became the first wolf recorded west of the Cascades since 1947, when the last known wolf was killed for a government bounty ④. Wolves once roamed across North America, but for centuries they were hunted and trapped by humans. By the 1960's, wolves remained only in Alaska, Canada, and northern Minnesota and Michigan.

In late December, 2011, Wolf OR-7 entered California, becoming the first known wolf in California since the last bounty was collected in 1924 ⑤. With government protection from the Endangered Species Act, wolves, like OR-7, are slowly returning across the U.S. ⑥. To help wolf populations recover, wolves were reintroduced to Idaho from Canada in 1995-96. Wolf OR-7's parents are descendants of these wolves, but other wolves also continue to disperse from Canada on their own.

After about a year in California, Wolf OR-7 settled in Southern Oregon. He was joined by a female wolf linked to Northeast Oregon. In the spring of 2014 they gave birth to at least three pups ⑦.

In wolf packs, adults share the responsibility of raising pups. Pups venture from the den in summer to learn how to hunt and scavenge. Wolves hunt for whatever food is available, often deer, elk and beaver in the Northwest. What they don't eat becomes food for ravens, bears and other animals.

OR-7's family is named the Rogue Pack, after the Rogue River. As the pack grows, and his pups disperse, where do you think they may go?

This story map created by the OR-7 Expedition (used with their permission) shows Journey's route and tells the tale of his remarkable trip.

The story of Oregon's famous wandering

Wolf OR-7

ILLUSTRATION CREDITS

BY PAGE NUMBER

1   *Walking wolf illustration*: Courtesy of Hannah Hartsell.

6   *Beaver illustration*: Courtesy of George Bumann.

11   *Walking wolf illustration*: Courtesy of Hannah Hartsell.

12   *Running wolf illustration*: Courtesy of Jane Elgin.

16   *Wolf and elk illustration*: Courtesy of Helen Patti Hill.

18   *Howling wolf illustration*: Courtesy of Hannah Hartsell.

23   *Walking wolf illustration*: Courtesy of Hannah Hartsell.

29   *Moose illustration*: Courtesy of George Bumann.

39   *Walking wolf illustration*: Courtesy of Hannah Hartsell.

41   *Black wolf illustration:* Courtesy of George Bumann.

45   *Wolf pup illustration*: Courtesy of Jane Elgin.

48   *Standing wolf illustration*: Courtesy of Hannah Hartsell.

54   *Deer illustration*: Courtesy of Helen Patti Hill.

54   *Gray and black wolves illustration*: Courtesy of George Bumann.

57   *Walking wolf illustration*: Courtesy of Hannah Hartsell.

ACKNOWLEDGMENTS

One does not create a book like this without a lot of help, at least not this writer! Thank you to my three wonderful kids, Hannah, Megan, and Dylan, for their input and support on this project. My appreciation extends to my family in the Midwest, including my mother, Jane Elgin, and my father, Robert Elgin. My dad left this world in 2010, but his inspiration will never fade. Many thanks to those who read all or parts of this work and added suggestions and encouragement. These folks include: Ann Barton, Roblyn Brown, Pam and Randy Comeleo, Elisabeth Cravens, John Darling, Bruce and Erin Elgin, Michelle Elgin, Helen Patti Hill, Lilia Letsch, Rob Klavins, Karen Kovacs, Rebecca Olien, Russell Page, Liz Parrish, Wally Sykes, Mark Vargas, and Amaroq Weiss. Thanks to George Bumann, Jane Elgin, Hannah Hartsell, and Helen Patti Hill for the beautiful illustrations that add so much to this book. I want to acknowledge the dedication and hard work of the biologists with the Oregon Department of Fish and Wildlife, the California Department of Fish and Wildlife, and the US Fish and Wildlife Service. Thanks to them also for posting their photos of wolves and allowing use of these pictures. Lastly, my gratitude goes out to the many selfless individuals who continue, even when it's not easy, to stick their necks out to protect the ever-controversial wolf.

INDEX

ABOUT THE AUTHOR

Beckie Elgin grew up in a zoo her father directed in Iowa, where she helped care for all kinds of animals, including wolves. Since then, she has raised a family and earned degrees in Environmental Studies, Nursing, English, and an MFA in Creative Writing. She writes fiction and nonfiction and has been published in *Earth Island Journal*, *The Oregonian*, *The Tusculum Review*, *Litro*, *Horses in Art*, *The Bark*, and others. Beckie enjoys searching for wolf tracks and listening for howls in the mountains near her Southern Oregon home. Please visit her blog at https://wolvesandwriting.com.

This photo of me with a very affectionate three-year old wolf named Akela was taken at the Des Moines Zoo in 1974.

Summer days are hot in the Rogue Valley and his coat is thin and red-tinged, perhaps from the sun. His head is held low as though he's had a tough day. His back looks a little swayed. Maybe he is returning from a hunting trip, carrying food for his hungry pups in his belly. At seven years of age, this is an old wolf, and one that has not led an easy life. He must be a bit worn out, but as of June 8, 2016, when this trail camera photo was taken, Journey was still going strong.

CPSIA information can be obtained
at www.ICGtesting.com
Printed in the USA
BVHW020855160220
572247BV00001B/4